D. R. Lucas

Apostolic Hymns and Songs

a collection of hymns and songs

D. R. Lucas

Apostolic Hymns and Songs
a collection of hymns and songs

ISBN/EAN: 9783337089320

Printed in Europe, USA, Canada, Australia, Japan

Cover: Foto ©Lupo / pixelio.de

More available books at **www.hansebooks.com**

APOSTOLIC
HYMNS AND SONGS.

A Collection of Hymns and Songs, both New and Old,

FOR THE

CHURCH, PROTRACTED MEETINGS, AND THE SUNDAY SCHOOL.

By D. R. LUCAS.
Assisted by Z. M. PARVIN.

OSKALOOSA, IOWA
CENTRAL BOOK CONCERN.

PREFACE.

APOSTOLIC HYMNS AND SONGS has been prepared with the idea of presenting the Apostolic teaching, the Gospel, with all its facts, commands, and promises, in song, in such a manner that "sense and sound" may go together. Especial attention has been given to the adaptation of hymns and songs for protracted and social meetings that the whole congregation can sing, and the effort has been made to utilize the singing of the Sunday-school in the church, the author regarding it as a great mistake to make a distinction between church and Sunday-school music. The time to teach the plain, grand old melodies is in childhood, that in all after years the songs of childhood may be the songs of age, which can never be done with the "hop, skip and jump" music that is evanescent in its character and not adapted to congregational singing. Consequently many of the old melodies, those that have stood the test of public judgment, have been selected in preference to new ones. At the same time, a sufficient number of new hymns and songs have been prepared to give variety and interest in the work to those who desire something new, and the author flatters himself that many of them will meet with a hearty reception by those who appreciate pure, sweet, and scriptural songs. The department of music and harmony has been under the supervision of Prof. Z. M. Parvin, whose reputation as a composer and harmonist is a sufficient guarantee that this part of the work is well done. Credit has been given in the proper place to the authors of both words and music, as far as possible; and to the many friends who have contributed to these pages, we desire to express our thanks.

D. R. LUCAS.

Entered according to Act of Congress, in the year 1875,

BY D. R. LUCAS,

In the Office of the Librarian of Congress, at Washington.

ELECTROTYPED AT THE FRANKLIN TYPE FOUNDRY, CINCINNATI.

APOSTOLIC
HYMNS AND SONGS.

PSALMS AND HYMNS AND SONGS.

D. R. LUCAS.   *Eph. v: 19 and Col. iii: 16.*   Z. M. PARVIN.

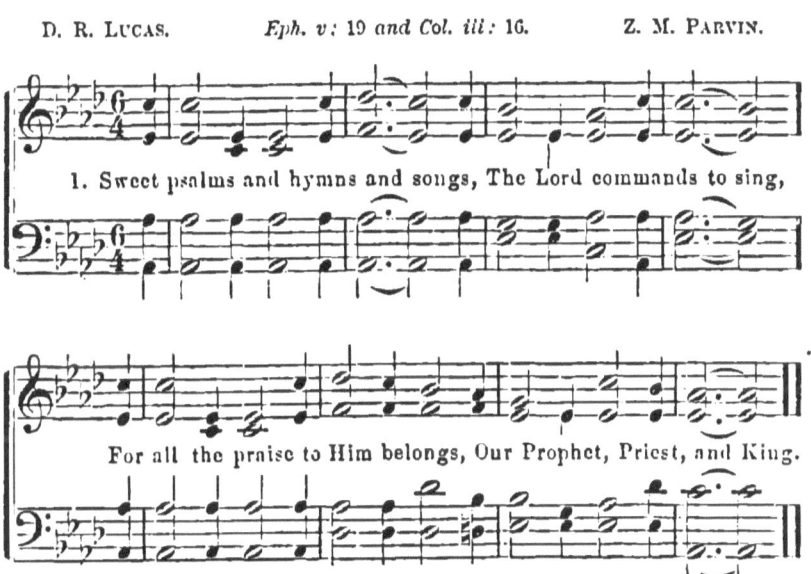

1. Sweet psalms and hymns and songs, The Lord commands to sing, For all the praise to Him belongs, Our Prophet, Priest, and King.

2 We lift our hearts to thee,
  With love our voices raise,
With sweetest strains of melody,
  Thy hallowed name to praise.

3 We let the Word of Christ,
  Dwell richly in our hearts,
And sing the tender love and peace,
  The Spirit there imparts.

4 Let all the saints of God,
  In Christ the Lord rejoice, [songs,
And join in psalms and hymns and
  With one united voice.

HEBRON: a Psalm. L. M.

D. R. LUCAS. DR. L. MASON.

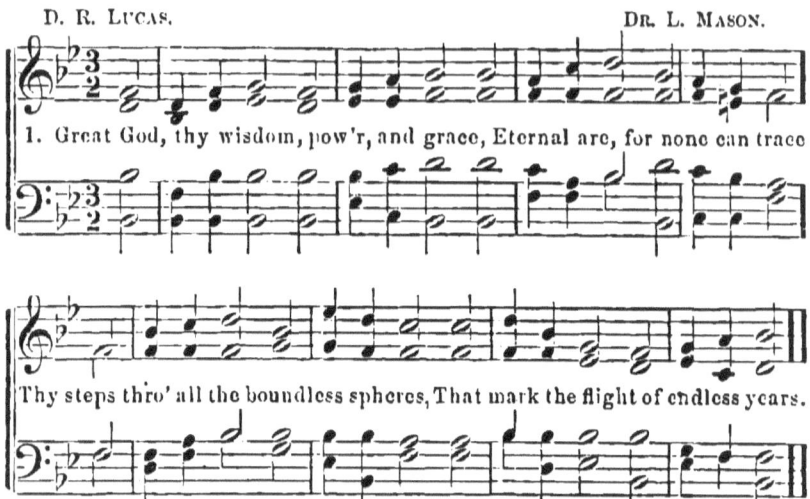

1. Great God, thy wisdom, pow'r, and grace, Eternal are, for none can trace Thy steps thro' all the boundless spheres, That mark the flight of endless years.

2 The heavens above thy pow'r declare,
Thy hand in guiding every star,
The sun and moon one law obey,
And wide thy sovereign might display.

3 No greater wisdom marks thy plan
In all thy works than reasoning man,
The gift of wisdom's ample store,
With mind to worship and adore.

4 Thy grace is seen in Christ the Lord,
Who was, with thee, Almighty Word,
Made flesh to manifest thy love,
In deeds that all thy favors prove.

5 Protect us, Father, by thy might,
By wisdom lead our steps aright,
Thy favor be our sweetest joy,
While psalms of praise our tongues employ.

Glorying only in the Cross.

1 When I survey the wondrous cross
On which the Prince of glory died,
My richest gain I count but loss,
And pour contempt on all my pride.

2 Forbid it, Lord, that I should boast,
Save in the death of Christ, my Lord;
All the vain things that charm me most,
I sacrifice them to his blood

3 See from his head, his hands, his feet,
Sorrow and love flow mingled down;
Did e'er such love and sorrow meet—
Or thorns compose so rich a crown?

4 Were the whole realm of nature mine,
That were a present far too small;
Love so amazing, so divine,
Demands my soul, my life, my all!
WATTS.

The power of God unto salvation.

1 God, in the gospel of his Son,
Makes his eternal counsels known;
'Tis here his richest mercy shines,
And truth is drawn in fairest lines.

2 Here sinners of a humble frame
May taste his grace and learn his name;
'Tis writ in characters of blood,
Severely just—immensely good.

3 Here Jesus, in ten thousand ways,
His soul attracting charms displays;
Recounts his poverty and pains,
And tells his love in melting strains.

4 May this blest volume ever lie
Close to my heart, and near my eye—
Till life's last hour my soul engage
And be my chosen heritage!
BEDDOME.

ALWAYS NEAR: a Hymn. C. M. 5

In him we live, and move, and have our being.—Acts xvii: 28.

D. R. LUCAS. MISS DELLA ANGLE.

1. Father of all, since thou art near,
In thee I live and move,
I cast away my every fear,
Rejoicing in thy love.

2 I can not see thy outstretched arm,
That guards my onward way,
But sheltered there from every harm,
No terror can dismay.

3 My being on the earth in thee,
Continues every hour;
And though Thy hand I may not see,
I trust its gracious power.

4 Why should I ever sing or say,
"Nearer, my God, to thee,"
Since thou art ever and alway
So very near to me?

5 All that doth intervene is sin,
Brok'n by redeeming grace,
Thy love has conquered self within,
Make there thy dwelling-place.

Endure hardness as a good soldier.

1 Am I a soldier of the cross,
A follower of the Lamb?
And shall I fear to own his cause,
Or blush to speak his name?

2 Must I be carried to the skies
On flowery beds of ease,
While others fought to win the prize,
And sailed through bloody seas?

3 Are there no foes for me to face?
Must I not stem the flood?
Is this vile world a friend to grace,
To help me on to God?

4 Sure I must fight if I would reign;
Increase my courage, Lord!
I'll bear the toil, endure the pain,
Supported by thy word.

5 Thy saints, in all this glorious war,
Shall conquer, though they die;
They see the triumph from afar,
With Hope's exulting eye.

6 When that illustrious day shall rise,
And all thy armies shine
In robes of victory through the skies,
The glory shall be thine.   WATTS.

With all boldness.

1 I'm not ashamed to own my Lord,
Nor to defend his cause,
Maintain the honors of his word,
The glory of his cross.

2 Jesus, my Lord, I know his name,
His name is all my trust;
Nor will he put my soul to shame,
Nor let my hope be lost.

3 Firm as his throne his promise stands
And he can well secure
What I've committed to his hands
Till the decisive hour.

4 Then will he own my humble name
Before his Father's face,
And in the new Jerusalem
Appoint for me a place.   WATTS.

THE FIRST SONG.

D. R. LUCAS. *Praising God.—Acts ii: 47.* Z. M. PARVIN.

1. Ancient church of Christ upraising, With a gladsome cheerful voice,
In their hearts their Savior praising, Who had made their hearts rejoice;
We can hear by faith the singing, First glad song and sweet refrain,
First by mortal tongue the singing, Jesus died, and rose again.

2 Song of prophets, ages olden,
　Sang Messiah, yet to come,
Now fulfilled the promise golden
　Christ had risen from the tomb;
And their hearts break forth in glory,
　Fear and care no more restrain,
For they sing the joyous story,
　Jesus died, and rose again.

3 Ever since adown the ages
　Men have raised their hearts in song,
Humble Christians, saints, and sages
　Each the joyful notes prolong;
For no other song comparing,
　Breaks the fear of death and pain,
Like the simple strain declaring
　Jesus died, and rose again.

THE OPEN DOOR. S. M.

I will give unto thee the keys of the kingdom of heaven.—Matt. xvi: 19.

D. R. LUCAS. Z. M. PARVIN.

1. The Lord to Peter gave, Before he left the earth, The keys to open wide the door That leads to heavenly birth.

2 The Holy Spirit came
  On Pentecostal day,
And gave by inspiration's tongue,
  The true and living way.

3 How Christ, the Lord of love,
  By wicked hands was slain,
And overcame his enemies
  By rising up again.

4 With pierced hearts they cry,
  "Ye men, what shall we do?"
The answer comes, 'tis mercy's voice,
  As Peter tells them true.

5 Repent and be baptized,
  If promise you would claim,
Remitted, then, your sins shall be,
  In Jesus' holy name.

6 Come, sinners, one and all,
  These terms to you are given,
No other way on earth is known,
  For this is bound in heaven.

My Charge. S. M.

1 A charge to keep I have,
  A God to glorify;
A never-dying soul to save,
  And fit it for the sky.

2 To serve the present age,
  My calling to fulfill—
Oh, may it all my powers engage,
  To do my Master's will.

3 Arm me with jealous care,
  As in thy sight to live;
And O, thy servant, Lord, prepare
  A strict account to give.

4 Help me to watch and pray,
  And on thyself rely,
Assured, if I my trust betray,
  I shall forever die. C. WESLEY.

He Wept. S. M.

1 Did Christ o'er sinners weep,
  And shall our cheeks be dry?
Let tears of penitential grief,
  Burst forth from every eye.

2 The Son of God in tears
  The wondering angels see;
Be thou astonished, O my soul;
  He shed those tears for thee.

3 He wept that we might weep;
  Each sin demands a tear;
In heaven alone no sin is found,
  And there's no weeping there.
  BEDDOME.

THE CHRISTIAN'S OPEN DOOR.

If you do these things you shall never fall.—2 Peter, i. 10.

D. R. LUCAS.   Z. M. PARVIN.

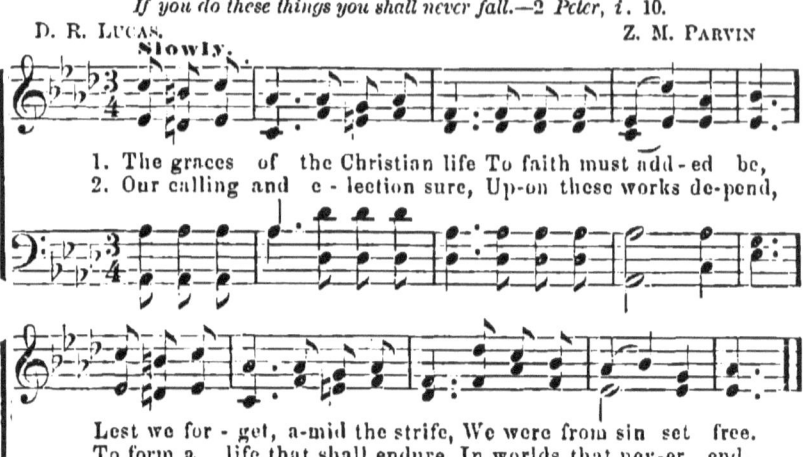

1. The graces of the Christian life To faith must add-ed be,
Lest we for-get, a-mid the strife, We were from sin set free.

2. Our calling and e-lection sure, Up-on these works depend,
To form a life that shall endure, In worlds that nev-er end.

3 Virtue and knowledge of the Lord,
Temp'rance and patience, too,
With godliness we keep the Word,
Good will to brethren due.

4 The crowning grace of all the seven,
The pure and peaceful love,
The last on earth tho' first in heaven,
Is found below, above.

5 Abundant entrance we'll receive,
When free from care and strife,
On earth our sins and sorrows leave,
And gain eternal life.

Union. C. M.

1 How sweet, how heavenly is the sight,
When those that love the Lord,
In one another's peace delight,
And thus fulfill his word!

2 When each can feel his brother's sigh,
And with him bear a part;
When sorrows flow from eye to eye,
And joy from heart to heart.

3 When, free from envy, scorn, and pride,
Our wishes all above,
Each can his brother's failings hide,
And show a brother's love.

4 Let love, in one delightful stream,
Thro' every bosom flow,
And union sweet and dear esteem,
In every action glow.

5 Love is the golden chain that binds
The happy souls above;
And he's an heir of heaven who finds
His bosom glow with love.
                 JOS. SWAIN, 1792.

---

1 Return, O wanderer, return,
And seek thy Father's face;
Those new desires which in thee burn
Were kindled by his grace.

2 Return, O wanderer, return;
He hears thy humble sigh;
He sees thy softened spirit mourn,
When no one else is nigh.

3 Return, O wanderer, return,
Thy Savior bids thee live;
Come to his cross, and, grateful, learn
How freely he'll forgive.

4 Return, O wanderer, return,
And wipe the falling tear:
Thy Father calls, no longer mourn;
'Tis love invites thee near.
               WM. B. COLLYER, 1812.

SOLID ROCK. 9

For other foundation can no man lay than that is laid, which is Jesus Christ.—
E. MOTE.   1 Cor. iii: 11.   Z. M. PARVIN.

1. { My hope is built on noth-ing less Than Je-sus' blood and righteousness;
     I dare not trust the sweet-est frame, But whol-ly lean on Jesus' name; } On Christ, the sol-id rock, I stand, All oth-er

2. { When darkness seems to veil his face, I rest on his un-changing grace;
     In ev-ery high and storm-y gale My an-chor holds with-in the veil; } On Christ, the sol-id rock, I stand, All oth-er

3. { His oath, his cov-en-ant and blood, Support me in the whelming flood;
     When all a-round my soul gives way, He then is all my hope and stay; } On Christ, etc.

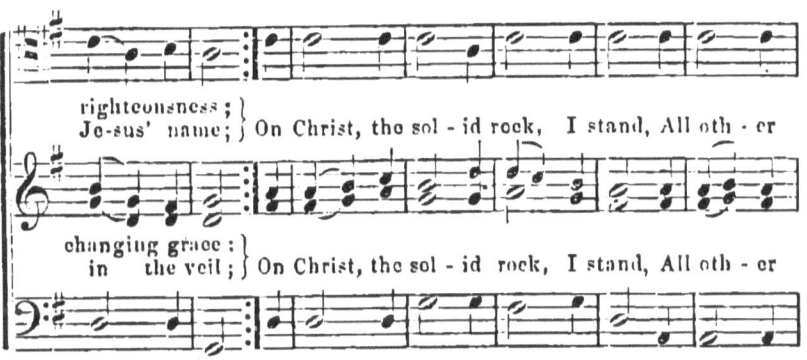

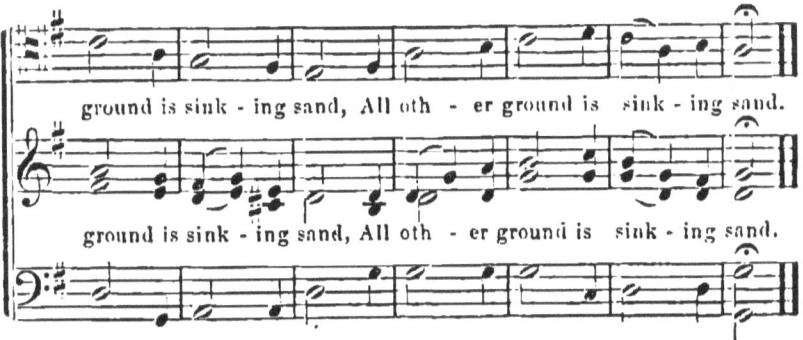

ground is sink-ing sand, All oth-er ground is sink-ing sand.

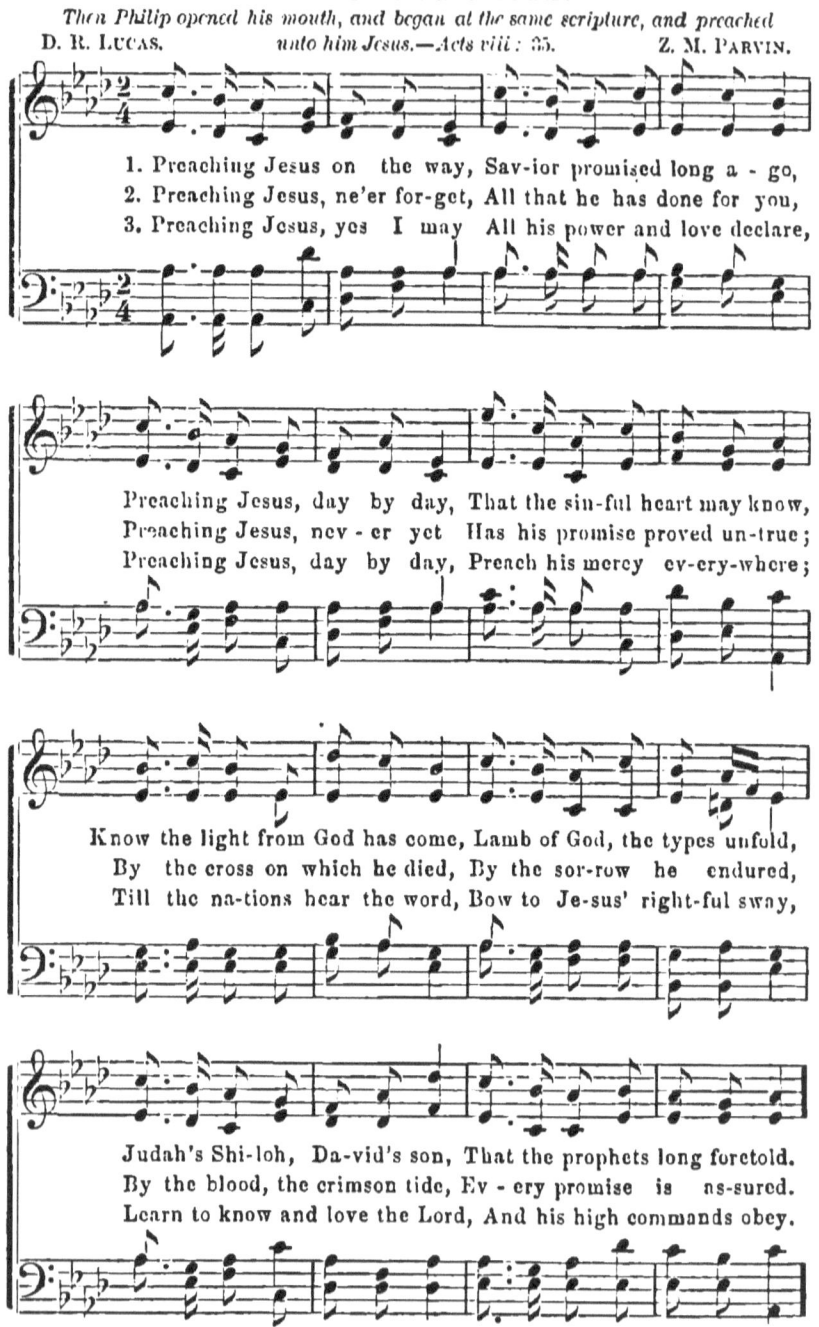

PREACHING JESUS. Concluded.

PLEYEL.

Death of a Christian.

D. R. LUCAS. — PLEYEL.

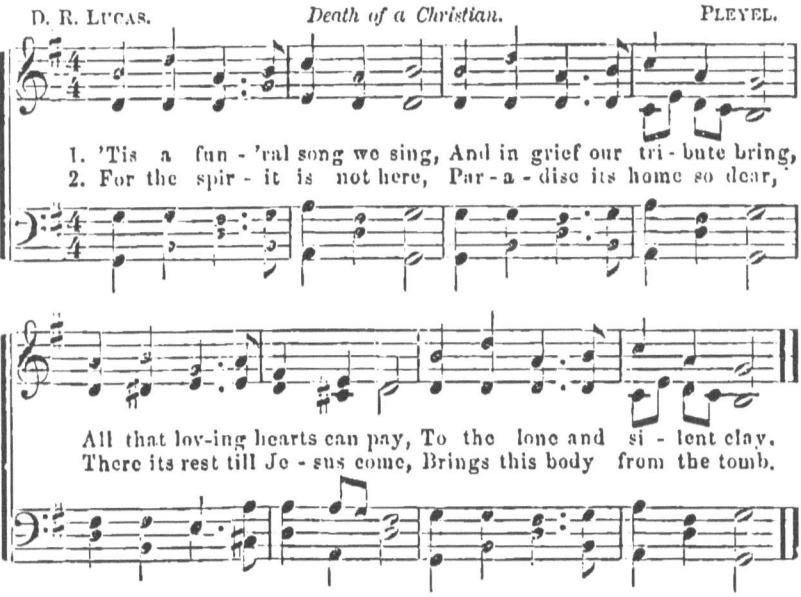

1. 'Tis a fun-'ral song we sing, And in grief our tri-bute bring,
All that lov-ing hearts can pay, To the lone and si-lent clay.

2. For the spir-it is not here, Par-a-dise its home so dear,
There its rest till Je-sus come, Brings this body from the tomb.

3 Reunited they will be,
Put on immortality,
Seek in heav'n their final home,
Where no death can ever come.

4 While lamenting then to-day,
Let us wipe our tears away,
And by faith the triumph see,
Death has lost his victory.

PRISONER'S SONG. L. M.

At midnight Paul and Silas prayed and sang praises unto God.—Acts xvi: 25.

D. R. LUCAS.   Z. M. PARVIN.

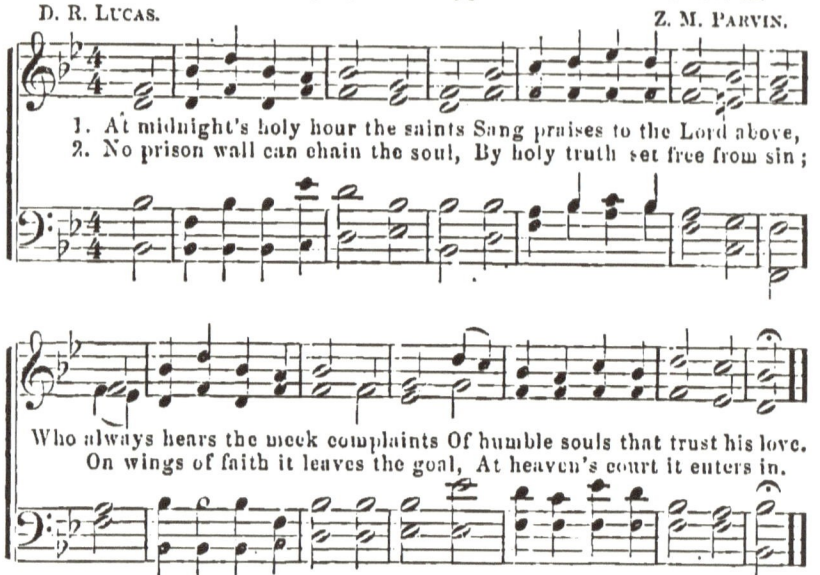

1. At midnight's holy hour the saints Sang praises to the Lord above,
2. No prison wall can chain the soul, By holy truth set free from sin;

Who always hears the meek complaints Of humble souls that trust his love.
On wings of faith it leaves the goal, At heaven's court it enters in.

3 And well they knew that God would hear,
For he is Father over all;
He rules and reigns in highest sphere,
And notes on earth the sparrow's fall.

4 An earthquake shook the prison door
Throws wide to freedom's fragrant air;
The loosen'd stocks declare no more
A worshiper should fetters wear.

5 Oh, let us, then, whate'er our lot,
Remember on our pilgrim way,
On downy couch, or prison cot,
In good or ill, to praise and pray.

---

1 From every stormy wind that blows,
From every swelling tide of woes,
There is a calm, a sure retreat;
'T is found beneath the mercy-seat.

2 There is a place where Jesus sheds
The oil of gladness on our heads;
A place than all beside more sweet,—
It is the blood-bought mercy-seat.

3 There is a scene where spirits blend,
Where friend holds fellowship with friend;
Though sundered far, by faith they meet
Around one common mercy-seat.

4 Ah! whither could we flee for aid,
When tempted, desolate, dismayed?
Or how the hosts of hell defeat,
Had suffering saints no mercy-seat?

5 There, there on eagles' wings we soar,
And sin and sense molest no more,
And heaven comes down our souls to greet,
While glory crowns the mercy-seat.

GROWING BRIGHTER.

By per. J. CHURCH & Co., pub.   Words and Music by G. T. WILSON.

1. As we wend our way to Canaan, Walking in the nar-row way,

Brighter still be-comes the glo-ry, Growing brighter day by day.

CHORUS.

Growing brighter, growing brighter, As we move a-long the way,

Growing brighter, growing brighter, E'en unto the perfect day.

2 Smiling faces brightly beaming,
  Soon, ah! soon must pass away,
But the pure, sweet light of heaven
  Is increasing day by day.

3 Earthly scenes of wondrous beauty
  Soon, alas, will all decay,
While the scenery over Jordan,
  Grows more charming day by day.

4 See that star! 'twas once all brilliant,
  Now it shines with feeble ray,
'Twill be lost in spreading daylight,
  In the light of perfect day.

FATHER, FORGIVE THEM. Concluded.

3 All the angels their watch-care are keeping,
And their harps, whose bright strings they were sweeping,
Are as silent as if they were weeping,
  For the One who, dying, can pray;
And we know there was wonder in glory,
As they whispered the sorrowful story,
For they knew there was no oratory
  Such a scene could ever portray.

4 O my soul! while that scene is appearing,
While by faith the sweet song I am hearing,
Let me cast far away all my fearing,
  For he dies to save us from sin;
"It is finished," he cries: oh, behold him,
As the sorrows of death now enfold him,
While the angels of God have enrolled him,'
  Only One who perfect hath been.

WESSELS. S. M.

D. R. LUCAS.   By per. S. M. LUTZ.

1. A-long the tran-quil path, Where ro-ses sweet-ly bloom, We pass in calm-ness on our way To-ward the si-lent tomb.

2 We know that God is love,
  His arms of mercy, wide
Extend to banish all our fears,
  And help us o'er the tide.

3 We feel that God is good,
  And tho' with care oppressed,
He will redeem us from the grave,
  And give the weary rest.

4 Within our trusting souls,
  A sweet and holy peace
Abides, and drives away our fears,
  And bids our sorrows cease.

5 Then rest, my soul, in God,
  Thy every thought he knows,
And he will give, if storms arise,
  A calm and sweet repose.

LOVE DIVINE.*

For God so loved the world, that he gave his only begotten Son, that whosoever believeth in him should not perish.—John iii: 16.

MRS. CLARA B. HEATH.   B. S. HOAGLAND.

1. Love divine! we see and won-der, How so pure a thing can be,
Love divine! we read and pon-der, On its wealth at Cal-va-ry.

CHORUS.
Love divine, Love divine, Love divine, Love divine.
Love divine, Love divine, Love divine, Love divine, love divine, love divine.
Love divine, love divine, love divine, love divine, love divine, love divine, 'Tis this love divine that beckons, From the cross of Calvary.

2 Love divine, that saves the sinner,
All unmeasured in its flow,
Reaching out beyond the human
Heights above, and depths below.

3 'Tis this love constrains and quickens
What is true and good in me,
'Tis this love divine that beckons
From the cross of Calvary.

From "Songs of Delight."

HOPE'S SONG.*

But if we hope for that we see not; then do we with patience wait for it.—Rom. viii: 25.

D. R. LUCAS. Z. M. PARVIN.

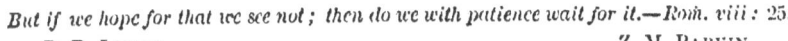

1. Hope on golden pinion brings us, From the far-off Savior's throne,
2. Bids despair and grief be broken, Care and sorrow to be gone;

Sweetest song in which she sings us, "It is bet-ter far-ther on."
By the magic words thus spoken, "It is bet-ter far-ther on."

CHORUS.

Ev-ery hour hope sings the song, Sings it with a joy-ful tone,

If we on-ly list and hear it, "It is bet-ter far-ther on."

3 How our souls are filled with glory,
By the prospect Hope makes known,
When she tells her rapt'rous story,
"It is better farther on."

4 Day by day we're drawing nearer,
Nearer to the great white throne,
And the blessed words grow dearer,
"It is better farther on."

* From "Songs of Delight."

18. RIGHT HAND OF FELLOWSHIP. 7s.

They gave to Paul and Barnabas the right hand of fellowship.—Gal. ii : 9.

D. R. LUCAS.   Z. M. PARVIN.

1. Children of the living one, With the Christian race begun,
2. Here we sit around the board, Table of our dying Lord,
3. With the hand we give the heart, Pledged to bear each one our part,
4. In our midst he stands to-day, In our hearts we hear him say,

As the Savior's voice you know, Welcome to the church below;
Eat and drink the tokens given, Of the bread that came from heaven;
In the union then we stand, Heirs with Christ, a ransomed band;
Sons and daughters of the Lord, If ye keep my holy word,

Here we meet to sing and pray, As we journey on our way,
You are welcome to the feast, Where the Master greets each guest,
Purchased by his precious blood, All anointed priests of God,
I will hear you when you pray, I will guard your path alway,

Here we keep the Master's word, Meet in love to praise the Lord.
Leave, oh, leave the world behind, Richer joys you here can find.
Sacrifice we offer here, For our King is always near.
Keep the promise I have given, Welcome you at last in heaven.

RIGHT HAND OF FELLOWSHIP. Concluded.

Fa-ther keep us by the way, Je-sus bless us all this day, By thy word and Spirit guide, Till we cross o'er Jordan's tide.

1 Children of the heavenly King,
As we journey let us sing,
Sing our Savior's worthy praise,
Glorious in his works and ways.
We are trav'ling home to God,
In the way our fathers trod;
They are happy now, and we
Soon their happiness shall see.

2 Fear not, brethren, joyful stand
On the borders of our land;
Jesus Christ, our Father's Son,
Bids us undismayed go on.
Lord! obediently we'll go,
Gladly leaving all below;
Only thou our leader be,
And we still will follow thee.

CEUNICK.

THE RIVER OF DEATH.

"*When I first became a Christian, the river of death appeared to be a very wide stream, now at fourscore years, it has narrowed to a rill that I can step across.*"—
Experience of Elder John Smith, of Kentucky.

D. R. LUCAS.   FRANK CHRISTIANER.

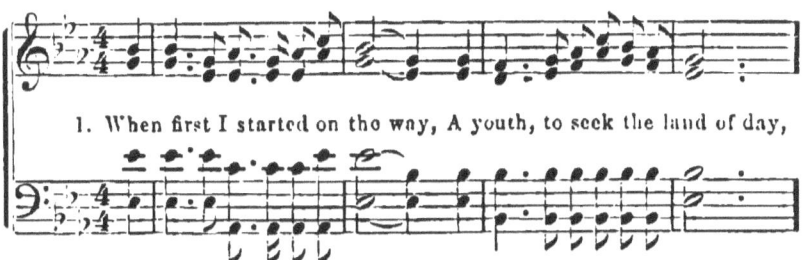

1. When first I started on the way, A youth, to seek the land of day,

THE RIVER OF DEATH. Concluded.

Death seemed a stream, a river wide, A darkly rolling billowy tide, On which great ships the waves might toss, My faith could hardly see across, The distant shore amid the gleam Was like a vision, or a dream.

2 But ere I reached my manhood's prime,
My faith had stronger grown with time,
And as I stood the stream beside,
The waves were gone, the rolling tide
Was flowing gently, and the shore
So close appeared, it seemed no more
A river wide, and hardly yet
It could be called a rivulet.

3 But when I came to riper years,
When earthly joys were mixed with tears,
My faith obtained a clearer look,
The stream had dwindled to a brook
So narrow that a bridge were vain,
To ford was easy and to gain
A footing on the other shore
So difficult appeared no more.

4 But now, when fourscore years are past,
And each on earth may be my last,
My faith in Christ is stronger still,
The stream of death is but a rill,
That I can step across, so near
The banks of paradise appear,
O God, I thank thee for this faith
That takes away the fear of death.

AMERICA.

The Spirit and the Bride say, Come.—Rev. xxii: 17.

D. R. LUCAS.   ENGLISH.

1. Come, sinners, come to-day, Why will you stay away From Christ, your Lord? The Master's voice, oh, hear, And cast away your fear, His love your heart will cheer, Obey his Word.

2 To-day the promise, blest,
To every humble guest,
  The call "who hears;"
The Savior gives so free,
That all to Christ may flee,
The King of Glory see,
  When he appears.

3 The Holy Spirit cries,
The Bride, the Church, replies,
  In Jesus' name
Why will ye fear the ill?
"For whosoever will,"
The living water still
  May freely claim.

4 Once more we ask you now,
Will you to Jesus bow,
  Your Lord to own?
Whose life a ransom gave;
No other power can save,
Redeem you from the grave,
  And give the crown.

5 The happy choirs above,
Who sing and know his love
  And righteousness,
Are waiting now to bear
The blessed tidings there,
That sinners, every-where,
  The Lord confess.

22. MY JESUS DIED FOR ME.

J. E. Rankin, D. D.
Z. M. Parvin.

1. My Je - sus died for me, Such love can I for - get,
Or e'er unmind - ful be, To whom I owe the debt?
On him my stripes were laid, He hung up - on the tree,
And thus my ran - som paid: My Je - sus died for me.

2. My Je - sus died for me? That was a sin - ner's doom;
He bowed in ag - o - ny, And lay within the tomb;
So great my in - ward guilt, My sins reached such degree,
For me his blood was spilt: My Je - sus died for me.

REFRAIN.

My Je-sus died for me, for me, My Je-sus died for me, for me,
And thus my ran - som paid, My Je - sus died for me.

MY JESUS DIED FOR ME. Concluded.

3 My Jesus died for me!
　The debt can I repay?
Lord, make me quick to see
　What most lies in life's way.
'Tis not enough to sing,
　Or pray on bended knee:
Life is love's offering:
　My Jesus died for me!

4 My Jesus died for me!
　And can my love grow dim?
Can I the trials flee
　I might endure for him?
Such love I'll ne'er forget,
　Nor e'er unmindful be
To whom I owe the debt:
　My Jesus died for me!

JESUS WEPT.

D. R. LUCAS.　　　　　*John xi: 35.*　　　　　Z. M. PARVIN.

1. At the grave of Laz-a-rus, Je-sus wept, Je-sus wept,
2. As we sing the mournful lay, Je-sus wept, Je-sus wept,
3. There's no oth-er words like these, Je-sus wept, Je-sus wept,
4. For they tell of love di-vine, Je-sus wept, Je-sus wept,

Sweet-est words he left for us, Je-sus wept, Je-sus wept.
How they fill our hearts to-day, Je-sus wept, Je-sus wept.
They will bid our sor-rows cease, Je-sus wept, Je-sus wept.
Kindness, mer-cy thro' them shine, Je-sus wept, Je-sus wept.

CHORUS.
Je-sus wept: be-hold his tears! Je-sus wept, Je-sus wept,
In them all his love ap-pears, Je-sus wept, Je-sus wept.

THE ISLAND. Concluded.

2 In that wonderful isle, as we sail on our way,
  Appears a bright mariner's goal,
Where the roaring of waves and the dashing of spray,
  Abide but in memory's scroll;
And visions of hope all its pleasures display,
The land where our kindred are happy to-day—
  We call it the "Home of the soul."
    We call it the "Home of the soul," etc.

3 In that evergreen isle with its great tree of life—
  "Twelve manner of fruits" it doth bear,
Every month in the year, and 'tis not like the waif,
  It needeth no guardian care:
No sickness or pain, no warfare or strife,
Are known in that land with sweet happiness rife—
  We call it the "Home over there."
    We call it the "Home over there," etc.

1 My gracious Redeemer I love,
  His praises aloud I'll proclaim,
And join with the armies above,
  To shout his adorable name.

2 To gaze on his glories divine,
  Shall be my eternal employ,
And feel them incessantly shine,
  My boundless ineffable joy.

3 Your palaces, scepters, and crowns,
  Your pride with disdain I survey;
Your pomps are but shadows and sounds,
  And pass, in a moment, away.

4 The crown that my Savior bestows,
  Yon permanent sun shall outshine;
My joy everlastingly flows—
  My God, my Redeemer, is mine.
    FRANCIS.

THE ROCK. 11s & 12s.

2 When Satan the tempter comes in like a flood,
  To drive my poor soul from the fountain of good,
  I'll pray to the Lord who for sinners did die—
  Lead me to the Rock that is higher than I!
      Higher than I, etc.

3 And when I have finished my pilgrimage here,
  Complete in Christ's righteousness I shall appear;
  In the swellings of Jordan all dangers defy,
  And look to the Rock that is higher than I!
      Higher than I, etc.

4 And when the last trumpet shall sound thro' the skies,
  And the dead from the dust of the earth shall arise,
  Transported I'll join with the ransomed on high,
  To praise the great Rock that is higher than I!
      Higher than I, etc.

CONFIDING TRUST. 7s. 8 Lines.

D. R. LUCAS.   Z. M. PARVIN.

1. Tho' the path be dark and cold, Clouds above may o'er me fly,
I can nev-er lose my hold, For my Lord is ev-er nigh.
Je-sus, Sav-ior thou art mine, Thou art all in all to me,
I will nev-er more re-pine, But will al-ways trust in thee.

2 All my life thy love has kept,
　From my childhood all the way,
While I've waked and while I've slept,
　Thou hast guarded night and day.
I will fear no coming ill—
　Death has lost his fearful might—
As I march up Zion's hill,
　To the land of glory bright.

3 Tho' thy face is still unseen,
　Tho' thy voice is never heard,
Through the veils that intervene
　Still I know thou art the Lord;
For thy word has come to me,
　Word of power and saving grace,
Treasured in my heart will be,
　Till I see thy smiling face.

4 Thou dost keep me, well I know
　That no other power can give
Blessings such as 'round me flow,
　While on earth by faith I live;
And should death, the tyrant, come,
　I will meet him face to face,
Angels kind will guide me home,
　To my Savior's dwelling-place.

PEACE IS MINE.*

Peace I leave with you, my peace I give unto you.—John xiv: 27.

Music by Z. M. PARVIN.

1. While I hear life's surg-ing bil-lows, Peace, peace is mine;
2. Ev'-ry tri - al draws him near-er, Peace, peace is mine;

Why sus-pend my harp on wil-lows; Peace, peace is mine.
D.S. Safe - ly he has sworn to guide me, Peace, peace is mine.
All his strokes but make him dear-er, Peace, peace is mine.
D.S. 'Tis a - gainst my sins he fighteth, Peace, peace is mine.

I may sing with Christ beside me, Though a thousand ills betide me,
Bless I then the hand that smiteth, Gently, and to heal delighteth;

* From "Songs of Delight," by per.

Love, Joy, and Peace.—Gal. v: 22.

1 What care I for fame's opinion,
   Love, love is mine;
Scorn and hate have lost dominion,
   Love, love is mine;
Anger's bonds no more enslave me,
Jesus died in love to save me,
And his Spirit freely gave me,
   Love, love is mine.

2 In my heart is Jesus reigning,
   Joy, joy is mine;
Banished thence is all complaining,
   Joy, joy is mine;
Wrath no more can 'round me hover,
Dark despair my future cover,
All my fears and doubts are over,
   Joy, joy is mine.

3 As a fruit of promised spirit,
   Peace, peace is mine;
Which the pure in heart inherit,
   Peace, peace is mine;
Peace at morn, and peace at even,
All my sins have been forgiven,
'Tis a foretaste here of heaven,
   Peace, peace is mine.

D. R. LUCAS.

WEBB.

Come over into Macedonia and help us.—Acts xvi: 9.

Words by D. R. LUCAS.　　　　　　　　　　　　　　　　　WEBB.

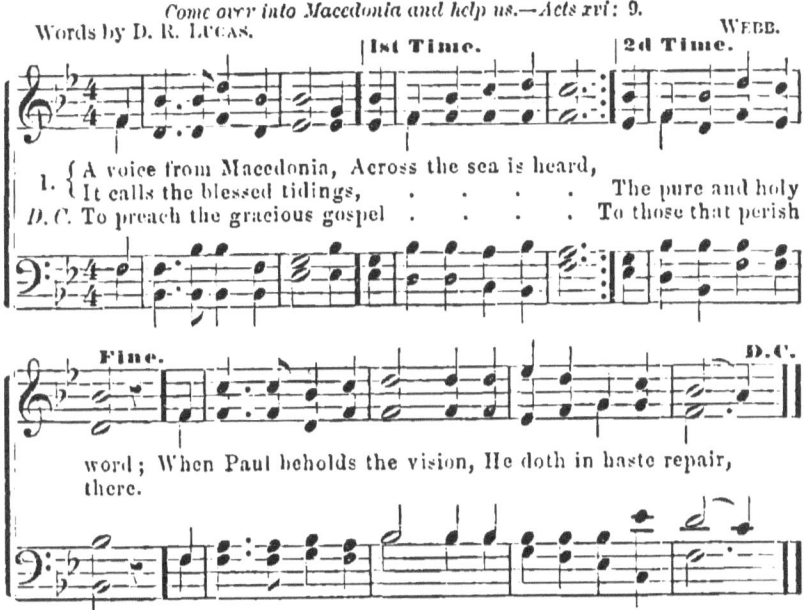

1. A voice from Macedonia, Across the sea is heard,
   It calls the blessed tidings, ... The pure and holy
   D.C. To preach the gracious gospel . . . . To those that perish
   word; When Paul beholds the vision, He doth in haste repair, there.

2 If we to-day would listen,
　That voice we all might hear,
Go preach the blessed gospel,
　The mourning hearts to cheer;
In every land and nation,
　Where sun and moon give light,
The voice of millions calling
　From error's darken'd night.

3 Awake, O Christian soldiers,
　Awake! Arise! Oh, send
The news of peace and pardon,
　Through Christ, the sinner's friend;
It is the Master's mission
　To all that love his name,
To bear the glorious message,
　And press the Savior's claim.

4 The church is the strong pillar
　Of truth and righteousness,
The means of God, appointed
　The world to save and bless;
Oh, let us then the freedom,
　That truth alone can give,
Proclaim to every creature
　That all my hear and live.

Song of our Pilgrimage.

1 Oh, when shall I see Jesus,
　And reign with him above,
To drink the flowing fountain
　Of everlasting love?
When shall I be delivered
　From this vain world of sin,
And with the blessed Jesus
　Drink endless pleasures in?

2 But now I am a soldier,
　My Captain's gone before;
He's given me my orders,
　And tells me not to fear.
And if I hold out faithful,
　A crown of life he'll give,
And all his valiant soldiers
　Eternal life shall have.

3 Through grace I am determined
　To conquer, though I die;
And then away to Jesus
　On wings of love I'll fly.
Farewell to sin and sorrow—
　I bid them both adieu:
And you, my friends, prove faithful,
　And on your way pursue.

4 And if you meet with troubles
　And trials on the way,
Then cast your care on Jesus,
　And don't forget to pray.
Gird on the heavenly armor
　Of faith, and hope, and love,
And when your warfare's ended,
　You'll reign with him above.

30. I DO BELIEVE.

And now why tarriest thou? arise and be baptized, and wash away thy sins, calling on the name of the Lord.—Acts xxii: 16.

Words by D. R. Lucas.   Old melody.

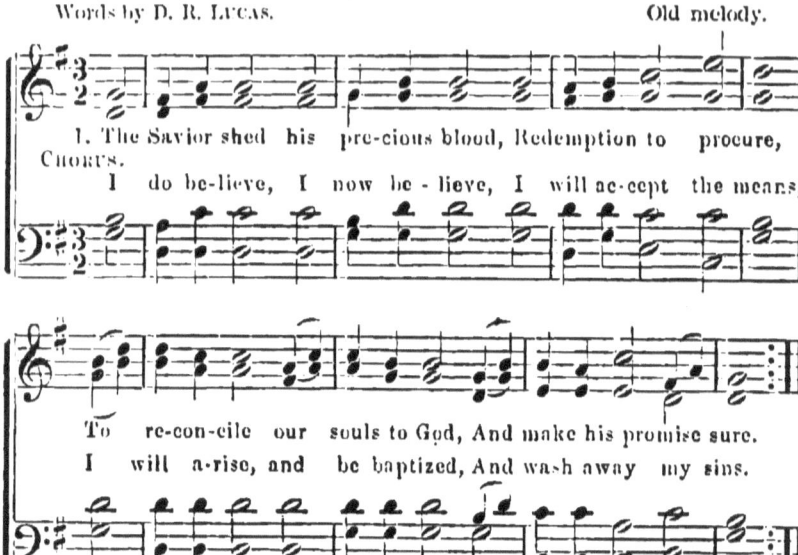

1. The Savior shed his precious blood, Redemption to procure,
To reconcile our souls to God, And make his promise sure.

CHORUS.
I do believe, I now believe, I will accept the means,
I will arise, and be baptized, And wash away my sins.

2 'Tis faith that purifies the heart,
   The faith that works by love,
That bids us from our sins depart,
   And all God's mercy prove.

3 Repentance leads us to confess
   That Jesus is the Lord;
Forsake our sins and wickedness,
   Obey his holy word.

4 We are baptized into the name
   Of Christ, the Son of God,
And thus exalted we may claim
   Redemption by his blood.

5 In all we do through good or ill,
   We will ourselves prepare
To do our gracious Father's will
   In humble contrite prayer.

Almost a Christian.—Acts xxvi: 28.

1 Almost a Christian, said the king,
   I am persuaded now
To be, and all my tribute bring
   To Jesus humbly bow.

CHORUS.
Oh, why not now to Jesus bow
   And full salvation claim?
A Christian be, from sin set free,
   And always wear his name.

2 "Almost a Christian," fearful pride,
   Persuaded now to be;
Almost a Christian, Paul replied,
   I would thou wert like me.
     Oh, why not now, etc.

3 Almost a Christian, can it be
   That this is all that you
Can say, since Jesus died for thee,
   And tells you what to do.
     Oh, why not now, etc

4 Almost a Christian, why not now?
   While it is called to-day
Forsake your sins, to Jesus bow,
   Walk in the narrow way.
     Oh, why not now, etc.

D. R. LUCAS.

DO NOT SAY TO-MORROW.*

Come, for all things are now ready.—Luke xiv: 17.

D. R. LUCAS. Z. M. PARVIN.

2 Do not say to-morrow, For to-day, Promised is salvation; Come, obey.
3 Do not say to-morrow, Time will be, You, perhaps, the sunrise Will not see.
4 Do not say to-morrow, God will save, You are swiftly passing To the grave.
5 Do not say to-morrow, I'll adore, For the Master's waiting, May be o'er.

RESPONSES.

1 I will be a Christian And receive Every promised blessing, He will give.
Chorus:
  With my heart, All my heart, I will confess my Savior, With my heart.
2 From my works of darkness, I'll depart, Jesus' love has conquered
                                                All my heart.
3 I believe in Jesus; He will bless, Those, who, humbly trusting, Sins confess.

* From "Songs of Delight," by per.

2 Better far a pure life in subjection to God,
　With a heart full of faith, hope, and love,
Than to walk with the careless and wicked the road,
　That the lovers of pleasure approve.
Sinner, turn to the Lord, then, for why will you die,
　Since Jesus the Savior says, come?
Tho' your sins are as scarlet fear not to draw nigh,
　He'll forgive you and bring you safe home.

BEREA. H. M.

The Bereans were more noble than those in Thessalonica, in that they received the word with all readiness of mind, and searched the Scriptures daily, whether those things were so. Therefore many of them believed.—Acts xvii : 11.

D. R. LUCAS.   Z. M. PARVIN.

1. The sinners of Berea Were noble called, for they
Examined well to see If Paul would lead astray;
They searched the scriptures day by day, To find the Christ
and learn the way, To find the Christ and learn the way.

2. With readiness of mind They heard th'Apostle's word,
Intent the truth to find About the risen Lord;
They searched the scriptures day by day, To find the Christ
and learn the way, To find the Christ and learn the way.

3 As faith by hearing comes,
  It led them to believe
In Christ, the promised one,
  That sinners would receive;
They searched the scriptures day by day,
:||: They found the Christ and learned the way. :||:

4 O sinner, would you know,
  What God hath done to bless
You on the earth below,
  And give you happiness?
Then search the scriptures day by day,
:||: For in them, God has taught the way. :||:

Missionary Hymn.

1 From Greenland's icy mountains,
   From India's coral strand,
  Where Afric's sunny fountains
   Roll down their golden sand,—
  From many an ancient river,
  From many a palmy plain,
   They call us to deliver
    Their land from error's chain.

2 What though the spicy breezes
   Blow soft o'er Ceylon's isle;
  Though every prospect pleases,
   And only man is vile:
  In vain with lavish kindness
   The gifts of God are strewn;
  The heathen, in his blindness,
   Bows down to wood and stone.

3 Shall we, whose souls are lighted
   With wisdom from on high,
  Shall we to men benighted
   The lamp of life deny?
  Salvation, O salvation!
   The joyful sound proclaim,
  Till earth's remotest nation
   Has learned Messiah's name.
              HEBER.

Rest for the Weary.

1 In the Christian's home in glory
  There remains a land of rest;
  There my Savior's gone before me
   To fulfill my soul's request.

Cho.—There is rest for the weary,
  There is rest for the weary,
  There is rest for the weary,
   There is rest for you;
  On the other side of Jordan,
  In the sweet fields of Eden,
  Where the tree of life is blooming
   There is rest for you.

2 He is fitting up my mansion,
   Which eternally shall stand,
  For my stay shall not be transient
   In that holy, happy land.

3 Sing, O sing, ye heirs of glory,
   Shout your triumph as you go;
  Zion's gate will open for you,
   You shall find an entrance through.

Parting Hymn. L. M.

1 My Christian friends in bonds of love,
  Whose hearts the sweetest union prove;
  Your friendship's like the strongest band,
  Yet we must take the parting hand.

2 Your presence sweet, our union dear,
  What joys we feel together here!
  And when I see that we must part,
  You draw like cords around my heart.

3 How sweet the hours have passed away,
  Since we have met to sing and pray;
  How loath are we to leave the place
  Where Jesus shows his smiling face!

4 O could I stay with friends so kind,
  How it would cheer my fainting mind!
  But pilgrims in a foreign land,
  We oft must take the parting hand.

5 My Christian friends, both old and young,
  I trust you will in Christ go on;
  Press on, and soon you'll win the prize,
  A crown of glory in the skies.

6 A few more days, or years at most,
  And we shall reach fair Canaan's coast
  When in that holy, happy land,
  We'll take no more the parting hand.

7 O blessed day! O glorious hope!
  My soul rejoices at the thought,
  When in that holy, happy land,
  We'll take no more the parting hand.

A Few More, Etc.

1 A few more years shall roll;
   A few more seasons come,
  And we shall be with those that rest
   Asleep within the tomb.

Cho.—Then, O my Lord, prepare
   My soul for that great day;
  O wash me in thy precious blood,
   And take my sins away.

2 A few more suns shall set
   On these dark hills of time,
  And we shall be where suns are not,
   A far serener clime.

3 A few more struggles here;
   A few more partings o'er;
  A few more toils, a few more tears,
   And we shall weep no more.
              BONAR.

THE OPEN GRAVE.

D. R. Lucas.   Z. M. Parvin.

1. I lay at night upon the ground, A little sleep and rest to crave, And when I woke at morn I found Myself beside an open grave. Then faith went back by mem'ry's sway, Where Jesus slept in Joseph's tomb, Where angels came and rolled away The stone, to scatter all our gloom.

2 When Mary and the women sought
   With spiced perfumes the Lord to lave,
They found the body gone and naught,
   Was there beside an open grave;
But turning 'round they saw the host,
   The smile of triumph on his face,
Proclaiming that king death has lost
   His triumph o'er the human race.

3 When death shall call me to his rest,
   When I have drawn my latest sigh,
And sleep in peace with all the blest,
   Hope whispers sweetly by and by,
When Christ, on resurrection morn,
   Shall come with power his loved to save,
I know that I once more shall stand
   Redeemed beside an open grave.

4 Oh, blessed hope, how sweet thou art,
   To free the soul from all its fears,
What joy and peace thou dost impart,
   Through all our toiling months and years,
While faith receives the present good,
   The pard'ning love of Jesus gave,
Hope bids us look beyond the flood,
   And stand beside an open grave.

* While in the army, the author retired one night (after a long march) without light and fire, and awaking at morn, found himself in a graveyard by the side of an open grave.

SUBMISSION.

Melody and words D. R. LUCAS.   Harmonized Z. M. PARVIN.

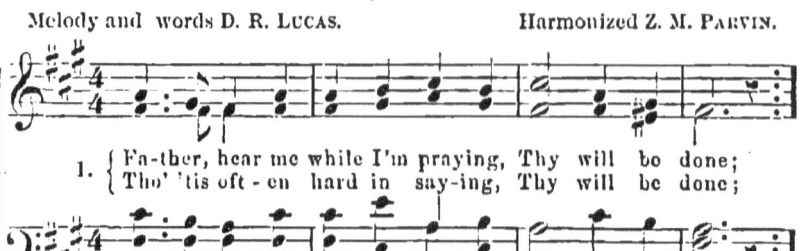

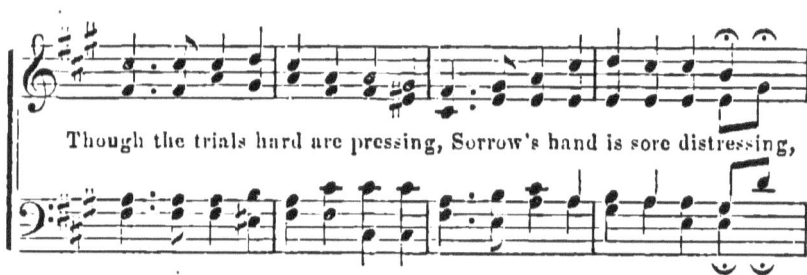

2 When the storms of sorrow sweeping,
    Thy will be done;
Scenes of anguish cause us weeping,
    Thy will be done;
We will cross the Cedron flowing,
With the suff'ring Savior going,
Hear him say, in anguish bowing,
    Thy will be done.

3 Give me poverty or treasure,
    Thy will be done;
Give me pain or give me pleasure,
    Thy will be done;
All the earthly good I cherish,
Let the brightest honors perish,
Still my heart thy love will nourish,
    Thy will be done.

4 Well I know thy power is ample,
    Thy will be done;
Make my heart thy holy temple,
    Thy will be done;
Then I'll say, on thee relying,
Faith and love my wants supplying,
While I live and when I'm dying,
    Thy will be done.

THE CLEANSING FOUNTAIN.

COWPER, 1779.   OLD MELODY.

2 The dying thief rejoiced to see
  That fountain in his day;
And there have I, tho' vile as he,
  Washed all my sins away.
    Washed all, etc.

3 Thou dying Lamb! thy precious blood
  Shall never lose its power,
Till all the ransomed Church of God
  Are saved to sin no more.
    Are saved, etc.

4 Ere since by faith I saw the stream
  Thy flowing wounds supply,
Redeeming love has been my theme,
  And shall be till I die.
    And shall, etc.

5 Then in a nobler, sweeter song,
  I'll sing thy power to save,
When this poor lisping, stamm'ring tongue
  Lies silent in the grave.
    Lies silent, etc.

TENDERNESS.

The Lord is very pitiful and of tender mercy.—James v: 11.

D. R. LUCAS.   OLD MELODY.

1. O my Lord thou art ten-der In thy pi-ty for me,
Where so oft I a sin-ner, Have sinned a-gainst thee.
D. C. It sheds a bright ha-lo Of light on my way.

How sweet thy for-give-ness, When hum-bly I pray,

2 From the days of my childhood
   Thou hast watched over me,
And an end of thy goodness
   I have yet here to see;
In joy and in sorrow,
   Thy love is my claim,
A kind, loving Father,
   Thou art ever the same.

3 I may be forsaken,
   My friends may depart,
Like Job I will trust thee—
   Oh, reign in my heart;
Thy words of sweet comfort,
   My hope and my stay,
Like a light from a beacon,
   Illume my dark way.

Over the River.*

1 Death's river is weeping,
   Its waters are cold,
Its dark, silent sweeping,
   Appalleth the bold;
Poor mortal hearts quiver
   When nearing its shore;
But across the dark river,
   Hearts sorrow no more.

2 Above the dark waving
   Hang clouds of despair,
And fearful storms raving
   Round passengers there.
With hope elevated,
   Faith views the fair shore,
Where the "just congregated,"
   Rejoice evermore.

3 For years and for ages
   The holy and good,
Thro' trials the sages
   Have passed the cold flood;
With earth's sorrows sated,
   They sought for the shore,
Where the "just congregated,"
   Shall sorrow no more.

4 The dear ones, so loving,
   Are passing away,
With angels are moving,
   They're singing to-day;
In light uncreated,
   Beyond the dark shore,
With the "just congregated,"
   With God evermore.

* Written by L. H. JAMISON, in reply to a letter of JOHN O'KANE.

HOME AT BETHANY.

Jesus loved Martha and her sister and Lazarus.—John xi: 5.

D. R. LUCAS.

1. I'll tell you a story of Jesus our King,
For under his banner of glory I sing,
He dwelt with the poor and the lowly while here,
In Bethany's village the humble to cheer.

CHORUS.
Home, home, sweet, sweet home,
For Jesus still loves all the humble at home.

2 When even around hung the curtains of night,
In a cot o'er the brook there was eager delight,
For Jesus went over in twilight to share,
Communion with those who would welcome him there.

3 If Jesus loved Martha and Mary while there,
And Lazarus, too, as the Scriptures declare,
He surely will love and will watch over me,
No matter how humble, how poor I may be.

Strangers and Pilgrims.

1 My rest is in heaven—my home is not here;
Then why should I murmur when trials appear?
Be hushed, my sad spirit, the worst that may come
But shortens thy journey and hastens thee home.

2 A pilgrim and stranger, I seek not my bliss,
Nor lay up my treasure in regions like this;
I look for a city which hands have not piled;
I pant for a country by sin undefiled.

3 Afflictions may try me, but can not destroy;
One vision of home turns them all into joy;
And the bitterest tear that flows from my eyes,
But sweetens my hope of that home in the skies.

4 Tho' foes and temptations my progress oppose,
They only make heaven more sweet at the close;
Come joy or come sorrow—the worst may befall,
One moment in heaven will make up for all.

LYTE.

STEPHEN'S VISION.

2 Look, ye saints! behold the gleaming,
  In the perfect land above,
Sure there is no idle dreaming,
  In the faith that works by love.

3 All around the throne is beauty,
  All is pure and holy there,
Angels fly on wings of duty,
  Faith perceives their tender care.

THE PIONEER'S SONG.

DEDICATED TO THE SURVIVING PIONEERS OF INDIANA.

"Our number is growing less very rapidly. Both the Littells, Longley, Wright, Smith, Newcombs, Campbell, Vawter and Thompson are gone."—Extract from a letter from one of the survivors.

D. R. LUCAS.   OLD MELODY.

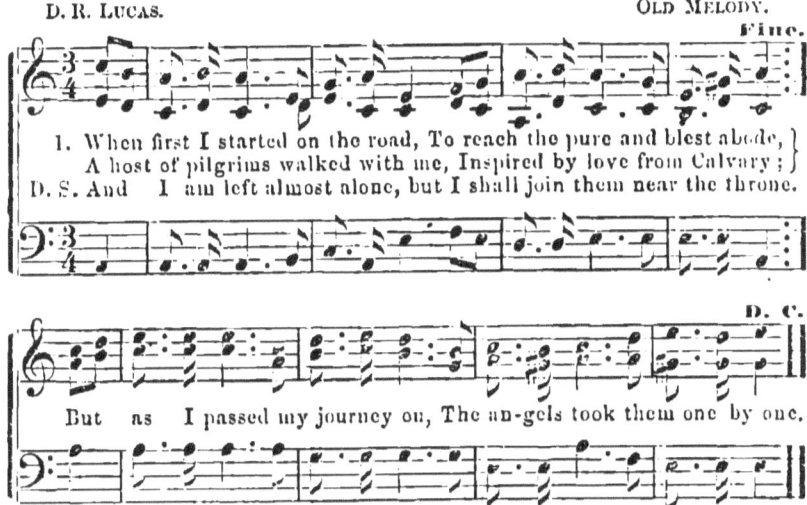

1. When first I started on the road, To reach the pure and blest abode,
A host of pilgrims walked with me, Inspired by love from Calvary;
D. S. And I am left almost alone, but I shall join them near the throne.

But as I passed my journey on, The an-gels took them one by one.

2 Tho' dear ones crossed the flood before,
While I still travel on the shore,
New comrades take the staff and join
To march along the heavenly line—
To join with me in sacred songs,
The praise that to the Lord belongs,
Who trod the path and taught the way
That leads us to the perfect day.

3 My pilgrimage will soon be o'er,
I see the Jordan just before,
A few more days of grief and care,
And I shall read the "over there;"
And as I sing this song to-day,
Inspiring hope doth sweetly say,
That I shall meet them all again,
And with them sing a nobler strain.

4 I've counted all below as dross
Compared with Jesus and his cross,
Content with what the Lord hath given,
My treasures are laid up in heaven:
Then shall we meet, with Jesus stand,
A reunited pilgrim band,
Lose all our grief, forget our pain,
And with the Savior ever reign.

Time Speeds Away.

1 Time speeds away, away, away,
Another hour, another day,
Another month, another year,
Drop from us like the leaflet sere,
Drop like the life-blood from our hearts, [parts,
The rose-bloom from our cheek departs,
The tresses from our temples fall,
The eye grows dim and strange to all.

2 Time speeds away, away, away,
Like torrent in a stormy day;
He undermines the stately tower,
Uproots the tree and snaps the flower,
And sweeps from our distracted breast,
The friends that loved, the fruits that blest,
And leaves us weeping on the shore,
To which they can return no more.

3 Time speeds away, away, away,
No eagle through the sky of day,
No wind along the hills can flee,
So swiftly or so smooth as he;
Like fiery steed from stage to stage,
He bears us on from youth to age,
Then plunges in the fearful sea,
Of fathomless eternity.

Just as I Am. L. M.

1 Just as I am—without one plea,
But that thy blood was shed for me,
And that thou bid'st me come to thee,
 O Lamb of God, I come.

2 Just as I am, and waiting not
To rid my soul of one dark blot—
To thee, whose blood can cleanse each spot,
 O Lamb of God, I come.

3 Just as I am, though tossed about
With many a conflict, many a doubt,
With fears within, and foes without—
 O Lamb of God, I come.

4 Just as I am, poor, wretched, blind;
Sight, riches, healing of the mind,
Yea, all I have, in thee to find,
 O Lamb of God, I come.

5 Just as I am, thou wilt receive,
Wilt welcome, pardon, cleanse, relieve,
Because thy promise I believe—
 O Lamb of God, I come.

6 Just as I am—thy love unknown,
Has broken every barrier down;
Now to be thine, yea, thine alone,
 O Lamb of God, I come.
          CHARLOTTE ELLIOTT.

Hinder Me Not. C. M.

1 In all my Lord's appointed ways
 My journey I'll pursue;
Hinder me not, you much-lov'd saints,
 For I must go with you.

2 Thro' floods and flames, if Jesus lead,
 I'll follow where he goes;
Hinder me not, shall be my cry,
 Though earth and hell oppose.

3 Thro' trials and through suff'rings too,
 I'll go at his command:
Hinder me not, for I am bound
 To my Immanuel's land.

4 And when my Savior calls me home,
 Still this my cry shall be—
Hinder me not—come, welcome death,
 I'll gladly go with thee.
          J. RYLAND.

"Them which Sleep in Jesus."—1 Thess. iv. 14. L. M.

1 Asleep in Jesus! Blessed sleep
From which none ever wake to weep,
A calm and undisturbed repose,
Unbroken by the last of foes.

2 Asleep in Jesus! O how sweet
To be for such a slumber meet!
With holy confidence to sing,
That death has lost its venomed sting.

3. Asleep in Jesus! Peaceful rest,
Whose waking is supremely blest;
No fear, no woe, shall dim the hour
That manifests the Savior's power.

4 Asleep in Jesus! O for me
May such a blissful refuge be;
Securely shall my ashes lie,
And wait the summons from on high.

5 Asleep in Jesus! Time nor space
Affects this precious hiding place,
On Indian plains or Lapland snows
The believer finds the same repose.

6. Asleep in Jesus! Far from thee
Thy kindred and their graves may be;
But thine is still a blessed sleep,
From which none ever wake to weep.
          MRS. McKAY.

"And Moses went up to the top of Pisgah."—Deut. xxxiv. 1. C. M.

1 Death cannot make our souls afraid,
 If God be with us there;
We may walk thro' its darkest shade,
 And never yield to fear.

2 I could renounce my all below,
 If my Redeemer bid;
And run, if I were called to go,
 And die, as Moses did.

3 Might I but climb to Pisgah's top,
 And view the promised land,
My flesh itself would long to drop,
 And welcome the command.

4 Clasp'd in my heav'nly Father's arms;
 I would forget my breath,
And lose my life among the charms
 Of so divine a death.
          WATTS.

SECOND COMING. 45

Behold, I come quickly. Amen: even so; come, Lord Jesus.—Rev. xxii: 20.

D. R. LUCAS.   MISS LIZZIE HULL.

1. Hear the words of Jesus spoken, Words the last he gave,
"I am coming, coming quickly, Those I love to save.

CHORUS.
We are ready for thy coming, While we watch and pray,
Welcome be thy great appearing, If it be to-day.

2 Long thy people, Lord, have waited,
   Waited patiently,
For the trumpet's blessed sounding,
   Trump of Liberty.

3 All the bodies of our kindred,
   In the grave await,
For thy voice to break the silence
   Of their lonely state.

4 With the great Apostle's answer,
   We would say, Amen!
"Even so;" Lord Jesus! welcome
   To the earth again.

5 Known the day, or known the moment,
   Is revealed to none;
But we wait in patience, saying,
   Lord, thy will be done!

TAKE ME BY THE HAND.*

Hold up my goings in thy paths, that my footsteps slip not.—Psalm xvii: 5.

J. B. SMITH, D. D.   Z. M. PARVIN.

1. Take me by the hand, my Father, For I do not know the way, Night-shades round me thickly gather, Hold me, else I go astray; Many are the ills betiding, Those who tread the way alone, Many are the foes conspiring—I would make thy ways mine own.

2. Toilsome is the way I'm treading, Hard and rough the dizzy height, Heavy are the mists o'er-spreading, And my home is out of sight; When I'm death's dark valley nearing, And approach the untried land, With the judgment day appearing, Take, oh, take me by the hand.

* From "Songs of Delight," by per.

TAKE ME BY THE HAND. Concluded.

Tune—"CHRISTIAN GRACES," page —.

The New Jerusalem. C. M.

1 Jerusalem, my happy home,
  Oh, how I long for thee!
 When will my sorrows have an end,
  Thy joys when shall I see?

2 Thy walls are all of precious stones,
  Most glorious to behold;
 Thy gates are richly set with pearl,
  Thy streets are paved with gold.

3 Thy gardens and thy pleasant greens
  My study long have been;
 Such sparkling gems by human sight
  Have never yet been seen.

4 If heaven be thus glorious, Lord,
  Why should I stay from thence?
 What folly 'tis that I should dread
  To die and go from hence!

5 Reach down, reach down thine arms
  And cause me to ascend, [of grace
 Where congregations ne'er break up,
  And Sabbaths never end.

6 Jesus, my love, to glory's gone,
  Him will I go and see;
 And all my brethren here below
  Will soon come after me.

There is a Land, a happy Land. C. M.

1 There is a land, a happy land,
  Where tears are wiped away
 From every eye, by God's own hand,
  And night is turned to day.

2 There is a home, a happy home,
  Where way-worn travelers rest,
 Where toil and languor never come,
  And every mourner's blest.

3 There is a port, a peaceful port,
  A safe and quiet shore,
 Where weary mariners resort,
  And fear the storms no more.

4 There is a crown, a dazzling crown,
  Bedecked with jewels fair;
 And priests and kings of high renown,
  That crown of glory wear.

5 That land be mine, that calm retreat,
  That crown of glory bright;
 Then I'll esteem each bitter sweet,
  And every burden light.

THE SAVIOR IS CALLING.

Hebrews iii: 7, 8.

Melody and Words by G. T. WILSON.   Arr. by Z. M. P.

1. Hark! the Savior now is call-ing, Loving-ly he bids you come;
   Now his words, like rain-drops, falling, Gently calls the wand'rer home.
2. See, the scep-ter is ex-tend-ed, Touch it, now, that you may live;
   Love and mercy in it blend-ed, Pardon, full and free, he'll give.

CHORUS.
Blessed tid-ings! joyful tidings! Hear, oh, hear Him while you may;
Blessed tid-ings! joyful tidings! Come, ye wea-ry, come to-day!

3 Follow not the world's fair bubbles,
   Like a baseless dream are they;
   Seek a balm for all your troubles,
   In the Christ, the living way.

4 Come to Jesus! life he'll give you;
   You shall think and want no more;
   In his church he will receive you—
   Lead you safe to yonder shore.

THROUGH THE NAME. 49

D. R. LUCAS.   Acts xi: 43.   Z. M. PARVIN.

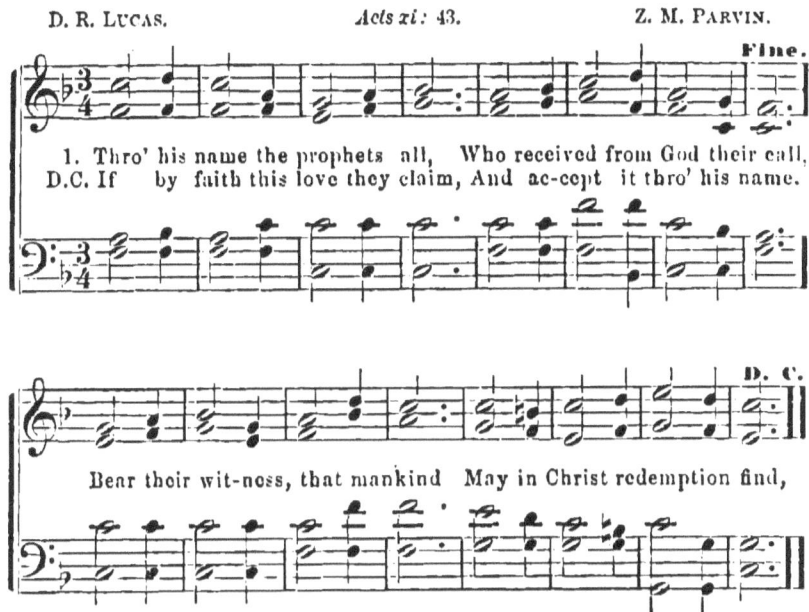

1. Thro' his name the prophets all, Who received from God their call,
D.C. If by faith this love they claim, And ac-cept it thro' his name.

Bear their wit-ness, that mankind May in Christ redemption find,

2 Thro' his name, if we believe,
What a blessing we receive—
Full salvation from the fears,
That in sin's dark cloud appears,
When we make our humble claim,
By obedience thro' his name.

3 Thro' his name whoever will,
How it doth our spirits thrill,
When we hear that all below,
Each his love and power may know,
Know that all may pardon claim,
By acceptance thro' his name.

4 Thro' his name, oh, doubt no more,
Mercy opens wide the door,
Oh, believe and enter in,
Leave behind your life of sin,
And the blessing humbly claim,
By obedience thro' his name.

Rock of Ages.

1 Rock of Ages, cleft for me,
Let me hide myself in thee;
Let the water and the blood
From thy side, a healing flood,
Be of sin the perfect cure;
Save from wrath, and make me pure.

2 Should my tears forever flow,
Should my zeal no languor know,
This for sin could not atone;
Thou must save, and thou alone;
In my hand no price I bring,
Simply to thy cross I cling.

3 While I draw this fleeting breath,
When my eyelids close in death,
When I rise to worlds unknown,
And behold thee on thy throne—
Rock of Ages, cleft for me,
Let me hide myself in thee.
              TOPLADY.

The Pearl of Great Price.

1 'Tis religion that can give
Sweetest pleasure while we live;
'Tis religion must supply,
Solid comfort when we die.

2 After death its joys will be
Lasting as eternity!
Be the living God my friend,
Then my bliss shall never end.

STEER STRAIGHT FOR US. Concluded.

2 He did so; and through the dark night,
   His boat reached in safety the shore,
And he clasped in his arms with delight,
   The forms of his darlings once more;
And oft he the story would tell,
   Relate it with boasting and pride,
How children once saved him so well—
   "Steer straight for us, father," they cried.

3 One bright day there came to the home,
   The king of the bier and the grave;
The children he claimed for his own,
   No science could lengthen or save
Their lives, and the children were laid
   Asleep in a grave side by side,
O'er which a rude marble displayed,
   "Steer straight for us, father," they cried.

4 The fisher heart-broken, alone,
   Pursued his sad, wearisome way,
Till death came to make him his own,
   The sting was all taken away.
And dying he told the sad throng,
   His angels had called o'er the tide,
The darkness is naught for their song—
   "Steer straight for us, father," they cried.

CORNELIUS. Concluded.

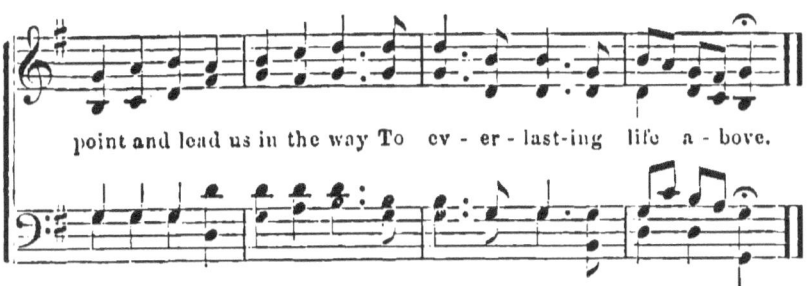

point and lead us in the way To ev-er-last-ing life a-bove.

The Eden Above.

1 We're bound for the land of the pure and the holy,
   The home of the happy, the kingdom of love,
Ye wanderers from God in the broad road of folly,
   Oh, say, will you go to the Eden above?
       Will you go, will you go,
   Oh, say, will you go to the Eden above?

2 In that blessed land neither sighing nor anguish,
   Can breathe in the fields where the glorified move,
Ye heart-burdened ones who in misery languish,
   Oh, say, will you go to the Eden above?
       Will you go, will you go,
   Oh, say will you go to the Eden above?

3 Nor fraud, nor deceit, nor the hand of oppression,
   Can injure the dwellers in that holy grove;
No wickedness there, not a shade of transgression;
   Oh, say, will you go to the Eden above?
       Will you go, will you go,
   Oh, say, will you go to the Eden above?

4 Each saint has a mansion prepared and all furnished,
   Ere from this clay house he is summoned to move;
Its gates and its towers with glory are burnished;
   Oh, say, will you go to the Eden above?
       Will you go, will you go,
   Oh, say, will you go to the Eden above?

5 March on, happy pilgrim, the land is before you,
   And soon its ten thousand delights we shall prove,
Yes, soon we shall walk o'er the hills of bright glory,
   And drink the pure joys of the Eden above.
       We will go, we will go,
   Oh, yes, we will go to the Eden above.

6 And yet, guilty sinner, we would not forsake thee,
   We halt yet a moment as onward we move;
Oh, come to the Lord, in his arms he will take thee,
   And bear thee along to the Eden above.
       Will you go, will you go,
   Oh, say, will you go to the Eden above?
                                R. L. COLLIER.

54. PRAYER FOR MILLENNIUM.

APOSTOLIC HYMNS AND SONGS.

Prayer for Millennium. Concluded.

2 Oh, come, then, thou bright angel, come,
 The Church of Christ, the Lord,
And preach the Gospel, pure and free,
 Thy chains the Holy Word,
To bind the great red dragon's power;
 With knowledge calm earth's fears,
Thy seal upon their forehead gives
 Men light a thousand years.

3 The world has long expecting hoped
 For time when war shall cease,
To greet the great millennial day,
 The dawn of perfect peace,
When earthly superstitions wild,
 No more excite men's fears,
Earth have but Christ's religion, pure,
 Throughout a thousand years.

4 Oh, come, thou faithful Word, and true,
 On thy white horse of peace,
And let thy gospel wide extend,
 Till wars and crimes shall cease;
Till o'er the earth, from pole to pole,
 Each man his altar rears,
And makes his heart an off'ring pure,
 Throughout a thousand years.

O Thou Fount of ev'ry Blessing. 8s & 7s.

1 O thou fount of ev'ry blessing!
 Tune my heart to sing thy grace;
Streams of mercy, never ceasing,
 Call for songs of loudest praise.

2 Teach me ever to adore thee,
 May I still thy goodness prove,
While the hope of endless glory,
 Fills my heart with joy and love,

3 Here I'll raise my Ebenezer,
 Hither by thy help I've come,
And I hope, by thy good pleasure,
 Safely to arrive at home.

4 Jesus sought me when a stranger,
 Wand'ring from thy fold, O God!
He to rescue me from danger,
 Interposed his precious blood.

5 Oh, to grace how great a debtor,
 Daily I'm constrained to be!
Let thy goodness, like a fetter,
 Bind me closer still to thee!

6 Never let me wander from thee,
 Never leave thee whom I love;
By thy Word and Spirit guide me,
 Till I reach thy courts above.
  ROBINSON.

Homeward. 8s & 7s.

1 Dropping down the troubled river,
 To the tranquil, tranquil shore,
Where the sweet light shineth ever,
 And the sun goes down no more.

2 Dropping down the winding river,
 To the wide and welcome sea,
Where no tempest wrecketh ever,
 Where the sky is fair and free.

3 Dropping down the rapid river,
 To the dear and deathless land,
Where the living live forever
 At the Father's own right hand.
  BONAR.

Look unto Me and be Saved.—Isaiah xlv : 22.

1 Come, you sinners, poor and needy,
 Weak and wounded, sick and sore;
Jesus ready stands to save you,
 Full of pity, love, and power;
  He is able,
 He is willing—doubt no more.

2 Let not conscience make you linger,
 Nor of fitness fondly dream;
All the fitness he requireth,
 Is to feel your need of him;
  This he gives you,
 'Tis the Savior's rising beam.

3 Come, you weary, heavy laden,
 Bruised and mangled by the fall;
If you tarry till your better,
 You will never come at all.
  Not the righteous—
 Sinners Jesus came to call.

4 Agonizing in the garden,
 Lo! your Savior prostrate lies!
On the bloody tree behold him!
 Hear him cry before he dies,
  "It is finished!"
 Sinners, will not this suffice?

5 Lo! the rising Lord, ascending,
 Pleads the virtue of his blood;
Venture on him, venture freely,
 Let no other trust intrude;
  None but Jesus
 Can do helpless sinners good.

6 Saints and angels joined in concert,
 Sing the praises of the Lamb,
While the blissful seats of heaven,
 Sweetly echo to his name.
  Hallelujah!
 Sinners now his love proclaim.
  HART.

OUR GOD IS THERE.

D. R. LUCAS.   Z. M. PARVIN.

2 While o'er our heads the thunders | loudly | roll,
Thro' clouds where vivid lightnings | now con- | trol,
The rainbow oft appears, a | token | fair
Of promise made, and speaks that | God is | there;
   Is there, is there, is there,
Proclaims with hope that God is there.

3 On Mount Moriah's rugged, | lonely | side,
Abraham offers up his | boy, his | pride,
The angel's voice breaks forth on | listless | air,
And speaks in tones of faith that | God was | there;
   Was there, was there, was there,
The angel speaks that God was there.

4 On Nebo's top where Moses | died a- | lone,
And passed away from earth to | land un- | known,
No human ear could hear his | dying | prayer,
And yet his burial speaks, that | God was | there;
   Was there, was there, was there,
His burial speaks that God was there.

5 On Calvary where the Lord was | cruci- | fied,
The voice of sweet forgiveness | when he | died,
That murmured faith, his last sad, | dying | prayer,
Proclaimed in sorrowing love, that | God was | there,
   Was there, was there, was there,
Proclaimed in love that God was there.

OUR GOD IS THERE. Concluded.

6 When thro' the gates of heaven at | last we | fly,
And tears are wiped from every | sorrowing | eye
By God's own hand, that raised us | from de- | spair,
We then shall see and know that | God is | there;
    Is there, is there, is there,
Shall know and feel that God is there.

SWEETEST THOUGHTS OF JESUS.

D. R. LUCAS.   GERMAN.

1. Sweetest thoughts of Jesus, Fill our hearts to-day, And we all must sing them In a gentle lay. Sweetest thoughts of Jesus, When he was a child, Loving, kind, and tender, Meek and pure and mild.

2. Sweetest thoughts of Jesus, While he dwelt below, How he gave his blessing, Full and free, we know; How he heard, in kindness, Ev'ry humble call, How he passed each moment, Doing good to all.

3 Sweetest thoughts of Jesus,
  Free from earthly pride,
On the cross forgiving
  Those who crucified:
How the grave he entered,
  How he rose again,
How he sent the gospel
  To the sons of men.

4 Sweetest thoughts of Jesus,
  How he rose on high,
How we all will greet him,
  Far above the sky;
How he'll bid us welcome,
  When our race is run,
Hear him say so kindly,
  Faithful child, well done.

AT JESUS' FEET. Concluded.

Let me, tho' most un-wor-thy, Sit down at Je-sus' feet.

The House of the Lord.

1 You may sing of the beauty of mountain and dale,
Of the silvery streamlets and flowers of the vale;
But the place most delightful this earth can afford,
Is the place of devotion, the house of the Lord.

2 You may boast of the sweetness of day's early dawn,
Of the sky's softening graces when day is just gone;
But there's no other season or time can compare,
With the hour of devotion, the season of prayer.

3 You may value the friendships of youth and of age,
And select for your comrades the noble and sage;
But the friends that most cheer me on life's rugged road,
Are the friends of my Master, the children of God.

4 You may talk of your prospects of fame or of wealth,
And the hopes that oft flatter the favorites of health;
But the hope of bright glory, of heavenly bliss—
Take away every other, and give me but this.

5 Ever hail, blessed temple, abode of my Lord!
I will turn to thee often, to hear from his word;
I will walk to thine altar with those that I love,
And rejoice in the prospects revealed from above.
W. HUNTER.

Precious Promises.

1 How firm a foundation, you saints of the Lord,
Is laid for your faith in his excellent word;
What more can he say than to you he has said,
You who unto Jesus for refuge have fled.

2 In every condition, in sickness, and health,
In poverty's vale, or abounding in wealth,
At home or abroad, on the land, on the sea,
As your days may demand, so your succor shall be.

3 E'en down to old age all my people shall prove
My sovereign, eternal, unchangeable love;
And when hoary hairs shall thy temples adorn,
Like lambs they shall still in my bosom be borne.

4 The soul that on Jesus has leaned for repose,
I will not, I can not desert to his foes;
That soul, though all hell should endeavor to shake,
I'll never—no, never—no, never forsake!
KIRKHAM.

KEEP THE PATH. Concluded.

3 Let us all in the struggle with sin be strong,
   Each join with glad heart in the rapturous song;
   Exhorting and cheering each other along
   In the ever bright pathway of life.

4 And when we have finished our journey below,
   The palm and the crown will the Savior bestow;
   To the haven of rest with the ransomed we'll go,
   Who have walked in the pathway of life.

CORONATION. C. M.

PERRONET, 1781.   HOLDEN, 1791.

1. All hail! the power of Jesus' name, Let angels prostrate fall; Bring forth the royal di-a-dem, And crown him Lord of all, Bring forth the royal di-a-dem, And crown him Lord of all.

2 You chosen seed of Israel's race,
   A remnant weak and small,
 Hail him who saves you by his grace,
   And crown him Lord of all.

3 You Gentile sinners, ne'er forget
   The wormwood and the gall;
 Go, spread your trophies at his feet,
   And crown him Lord of all.

4 Let ev'ry kindred, ev'ry tribe,
   On this terrestrial ball,
 To him all majesty ascribe,
   And crown him Lord of all.

5 Oh, that with yonder sacred throng,
   We at his feet may fall!
 We'll join the everlasting song,
   And crown him Lord of all.

Come, Humble Sinner.

 I Come, humble sinner, in whose breast
   A thousand thoughts revolve;
 Come, with your guilt and fear oppress'd,
   And make this last resolve.

2 Humbly I'll bow at his command,
   And there my guilt confess;
 I'll own I am a wretch undone,
   Without his sovereign grace.

3 Surely he will accept my plea,
   For he has bid me come;
 Forthwith I'll rise and to him flee,
   For yet, he says, there's room.

4 I can not perish if I go,
   I am resolved to try;
 For if I stay away, I know
   I must forever die.   JONES.

62   HOLD THE FORT.*

Suggested by Maj. D. W. Whittle.   *Words and Music by P. P. Bliss.*

1. Ho! my comrades, see the sig-nal Wav-ing in the sky!
2. See the mighty host ad-vancing, Sa-tan lead-ing on;
3. See the glo-rious ban-ner wav-ing, Hear the bu-gle blow;
4. Fierce and long the bat-tle rag-es, But our Help is near;

Re - in-forcements now ap-pear-ing, Vic - to-ry is nigh.
Might-y men a - round us fall-ing, Cour-age al - most gone.
In our Leader's name we'll triumph O - ver ev - 'ry foe.
On-ward comes our great Commander, Cheer, my comrades, cheer.

CHORUS.

"Hold the fort, for I am coming," Je - sus sig - nals still,

Wave the an-swer back to heav-en, "By thy grace we will."

* From "Gospel Songs," by per.

ARLINGTON. 63

Received ye the Spirit by the works of the law or by the hearing of faith?—Gal. iii: 2.

D. R. LUCAS.　　　　　　　　　　　　　　　　　　　　DR. ARNE.

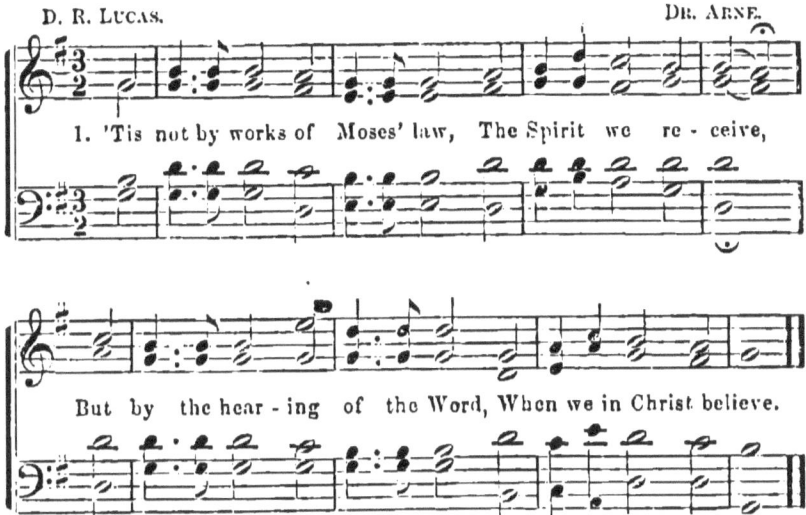

1. 'Tis not by works of Moses' law, The Spirit we re-ceive, But by the hear-ing of the Word, When we in Christ believe.

2 As faith in Christ by hearing comes,
　And hearing by the Word,
　We by the Spirit are convinced
　That Jesus is the Lord.

3 And thus it pleased our Father, God,
　Who plan of pardon gave,
　By preaching of the cross of Christ,
　Those who believe to save.

4 Oh, let us the engrafted Word,
　With meekness all embrace,
　The Spirit then will fill our souls
　With love and joy and peace.

He suffered, the Just for the unjust.—1 Peter iii: 18.

1 Alas! and did my Savior bleed?
　And did my Sovereign die?
　Would he devote that sacred head
　For such a worm as I?

2 Was it for crimes that I had done
　He groaned upon the tree?
　Amazing pity! grace unknown!
　And love beyond degree.

3 Well might the sun in darkness hide,
　And shut his glories in,
　When God's own Son was crucified
　For man, the creature's, sin.

4 Thus might I hide my blushing face,
　While his dear cross appears,
　Dissolve my heart in thankfulness,
　And melt mine eyes to tears.

5 But drops of grief can ne'er repay,
　The debt of love I owe:
　Here, Lord, I give myself away;
　'Tis all that I can do.
　　　　　　　　　　　WATTS, 1707.

Abounding in Hope.　C. M.

1 Since I can read my title clear
　To mansions in the skies,
　I bid farewell to every fear,
　And wipe my weeping eyes.

2 Should earth against my soul engage,
　And fiery darts be hurled,
　Then I would smile at Satan's rage,
　And face a frowning world.

3 Let cares, like a wild deluge come,
　And storms of sorrow fall,
　May I but safely reach my home,
　My God, my heaven, my all.

4 There shall I bathe my weary soul
　In seas of heavenly rest;
　And not a wave of trouble roll
　Across my peaceful breast.
　　　　　　　　　　　WATTS.

ACROSS THE SILVER SEA.

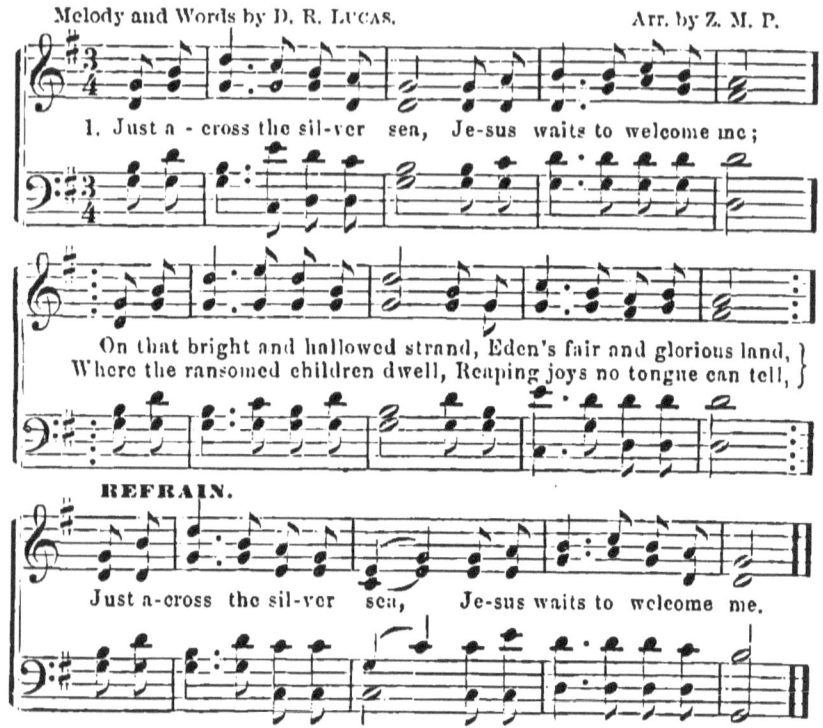

2. Just across the silver sea,
Jesus waits to welcome me,
In the city of his love,
New Jerusalem above,
Gates of pearl and streets of gold—
There I shall his face behold.

3. Just across the silver sea,
Jesus waits to welcome me,
To a mansion bright and fair,
He went over to prepare,
He will bring me by and by,
To his Father's house on high.

The Heavenly Country.—Heb. xi: 16.
Tune—"SWEET BY AND BY."

1 We have heard of a land far away,
Where the mountains and valleys of green,
Never know aught of death or decay,
Where no night casts a pall o'er the scene.

Chorus.—We shall go, by and by,
O'er those mountains and valleys to roam,
We shall go, by and by,
And will make that bright country our home.

2 We have heard of a heavenly clime,
Where the river of life ever flows,
Through the street where the temple sublime,
Does in grandeur and beauty repose.

3 We have heard that our Savior is there,
And our friends who have passed on before,
That they know not a sorrow or care,
And rejoice that their trials are o'er.   D. R. LUCAS.

MANY MANSIONS.

In my Father's house are many mansions.

JULIA A. GRAY.   GEORGE B. CRAWFORD.

1. Tho' cost-ly, beau-ti-ful, and grand, Mansions of earth may be, Where love and joy go hand in hand, With peace and u-ni-ty.

CHORUS. My mansion is not made with hands, Its grace no eye hath seen, It stands before the great white throne, 'Mid fields of living green.

2 Yet, by the eye of faith, I see
  Mansions more grand by far
Than palaces of earth can be,
  Tho' naught their beauty mar.

3 My title to it is secure,
  Gift of his dying love,
His blood alone can make me pure,
  Fit for that home above.

JESUS LOVES EVEN ME.

Words and Music by P. P. BLISS.

1. I am so glad that our Father in heaven, Tells of his love in the Book he has given;
Wonderful things in the Bible I see, This is the dearest that Jesus loves me.

CHORUS.
I am so glad that Jesus loves me, Jesus loves me, Jesus loves me, I am so glad that Jesus loves me, Jesus loves even me.

2 Tho' I forget him and wander away,
Kindly he follows wherever I stray;
Back to his dear loving arms would I flee,
When I remember that Jesus loves me.

3 Oh, if there's only one song I can sing,
When in his beauty I see the great King,
This shall my song in eternity be,
Oh, what a wonder that Jesus loves me.

* From "Gospel Songs," by per.

ST. THOMAS. S. M.

D. R. LUCAS.   A. WILLIAMS, 1770.

1. All things shall work for good, To those who love the Lord,
2. All things shall work for good, To those who heed his call,

And in a con-trite, prayerful mood, Obey his ho-ly word.
With God's great purpose un-derstood, Crown Jesus Lord of all.

3 All things shall work for good;
   Yes, all things here below;
E'en sorrow, rightly understood,
   May good, not evil, show.

4 All things shall work for good,
   A precious promise given,
To feast our souls with richest food,
   That God extends from heaven.

Now is our Salvation Nearer.

1 A sweetly solemn thought,
   Comes to me o'er and o'er,
To-day I'm nearer to my home
   Than e'er I've been before.

2 Nearer my Father's house,
   Where many mansions be,
And nearer to the great white throne,
   Nearer the crystal sea;

3 Nearer the bound of life,
   Where falls my burden down;
Nearer to where I leave my cross,
   And where I gain my crown.

4 Savior, confirm my trust,
   Complete my faith in thee;
And let me feel as if I stood
   Close on eternity;

5 Feel as if now my feet
   Were slipping o'er the brink;
For I may now be nearer home,
   Much nearer than I think.

                    ALICE CAREY.

Nearer to Thee.

1 Nearer, my God, to thee,
   Nearer to thee,
E'en tho' it be a cross
   That raiseth me;
Still all my song shall be,
Nearer, my God, to thee,
   Nearer to thee.

2 Tho' like the wanderer,
   The sun gone down,
Darkness be over me,
   My rest a stone;
Yet in my dreams I'd be
Nearer, my God, to thee,
   Nearer to thee.

3 There let the way appear,
   Steps unto heaven;
All that thou sendest me
   In mercy given;
Angels to beckon me
Nearer, my God, to thee,
   Nearer to thee.

4 Then, with my waking thoughts,
   Bright with thy praise,
Out of my stony griefs
   Bethel I'll raise;
So by my woes to be
Nearer, my God, to thee,
   Nearer to thee.

               MRS. S. F. ADAMS, 1841.

68 PERFECT UNITY. S. M.

D. R. LUCAS. *Read Eph. iv: 3-6.* Z. M. PARVIN.

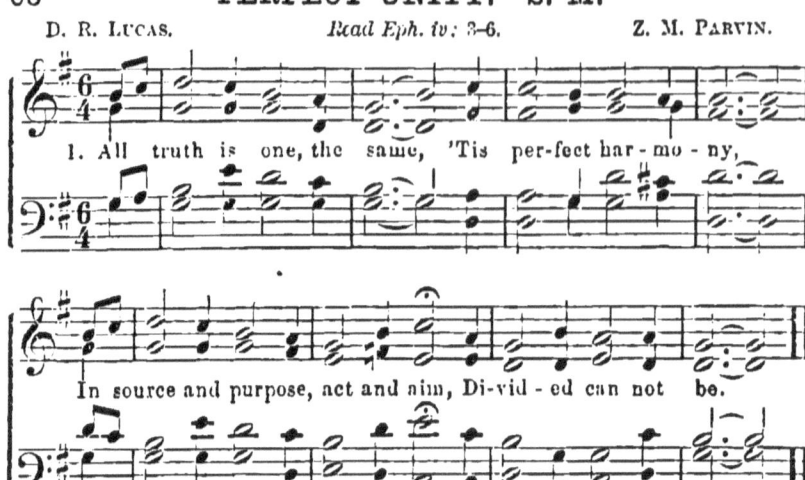

1. All truth is one, the same, 'Tis perfect harmony, In source and purpose, act and aim, Divided can not be.

2 We thus can understand
　The Savior's dying plea,
The Spirit's charge and great command
　For perfect unity.

3 One body of the Lord,
　One Spirit dwelling there,
One hope of gaining the reward,
　One calling to prepare.

4 One Lord, for aye the same,
　One faith in that one Lord,
One baptism in his holy name,
　Unite with one accord.

5 One God on whom we call,
　Who dwells within, above,
The great good Father over all,
　Whose one great name is love.

It shall stand forever.—Dan. ii: 44.

1 Thy kingdom, gracious Lord,
　Shall never pass away;
Firm as thy truth it still shall stand,
　When earthly thrones decay.

2 Thy people here have found,
　Thro' many weary years,
The sweet communion, joy, and peace,
　To banish all their fears.

3 And now while in thy courts,
　Do thou our love increase;
Give us the food our spirits need,
　And fill our hearts with peace.
　　　　　　　　W. T. MOORE.

Sighing for Rest.

1 O where shall rest be found,
　Rest for the weary soul?
'Twere vain the ocean depths to sound,
　Or pierce to either pole.

2 The world can never give
　The bliss for which we sigh;
'Tis not the whole of life to live,
　Nor all of death to die.

3 Beyond this vale of tears,
　There is a life above,
Unmeasured by the flight of years;
　And all that life is love.
　　　　　　　　MONTGOMERY.

I Love thy Kingdom, Lord.

1 I love thy kingdom, Lord—
　The house of thine abode,
The church our blest Redeemer saved
　With his own precious blood.

2 I love thy church, O God!
　Her walls before thee stand,
Dear as the apple of thine eye,
　And graven on thy hand.

3 For her my tears shall fall;
　For her my prayers ascend;
To her my care and toils be given,
　Till toils and cares shall end.

4 Sure as thy truth shall last,
　To Zion shall be given
The brightest glories earth can yield,
　And brighter bliss of heaven.
　　　　　　　　DWIGHT.

LORD, WHAT WILT THOU HAVE ME TO DO? 69

And trembling and astounded said, Lord, what wilt thou have me to do?—Acts ix: 6.

MISS M. G. DANFORTH.　　　　　　　　　　　　Z. M. PARVIN.

1. I came unto him in the morning, When the day was fresh and fair;
To-day I will work in thy vineyard, Was my heart's out-gushing prayer.

REFRAIN.
What wilt thou have me to do, Lord? Oh, what wilt thou have me to do?
What wilt thou have me to do, Lord? Oh, what wilt thou have me to do?

2 I came in the early morning,
　As the sun began to shine,
And now, and now it is evening,
　And the fruit still bends the vine.
　　What have I done for thee, etc.

3 I came unto him in the seed-time,
　When the spring was green and new,
Saying, I will sow with thy servants,
　For the lab'rers are but few.
　　What wilt thou have me to do, etc.

4 I came unto him in the seed-time,
　In the time of the bursting leaves,
And now, and now it is harvest,
　And where, oh, where are my sheaves?
　　What have I done for thee, etc.

NOT MY WILL.*

D. R. Lucas.   Z. M. Parvin.

1. I oft by faith have gone to see, The scene in dark Gethsemane, To hear the voice of Jesus pray, O Father, take this cup away, Yet, if I must endure alone, "Thy will, O God! not mine, be done," "Thy will, O God! not mine, be done!"

2. I saw a sinner, burdened down With weight of sin to bear alone, The Gospel message bade him see The scene in dark Gethsemane, I heard him say, the vict'ry won, "Thy will, etc.

3. I saw a Christian mother turn With tearful eyes to see the urn, That held the form of lifeless child, The angels claimed while undefiled, With breaking heart I heard her moan, "Thy will, etc.

4 I saw a Christian passing down
Death's valley dark without a groan,
Without a tear, without a sigh,
With faith in God, with Jesus nigh,
I heard him say, ere he was gone,
"Thy will, O God! not mine, be done."

5 O hasten, Lord, the glorious day,
When all shall own thy righteous sway,
Each angel bright thro' all the sky,
Each soul on earth take up the cry,
Thy wisdom, Lord, we each must own;
"Thy will, O God! not mine, be done."

* From "Songs of Delight," by per.

SOME DAY AT HOME. 71

D. R. LUCAS.   Partly comp. by Z. M. PARVIN.

1. "Some day," we say, and turn our eyes Up to the gates of Para-dise,
2. "Some day," we say, and sadly lay Our dear ones in the grave away,

Some day I'll be with Je-sus there, And all his bliss e-ter-nal share.
Some day we'll see and clasp their hands, In yonder bright immortal lands.

CHORUS.

Some day, some time, some hour I'll be At home, my Savior, home with thee,

At home, at home,

Some day, some time, some hour I'll be At home, my Savior, home with thee.

3 "Some day," we say, and sweetly sing
The triumphs of our Savior King,
Some day, sweet hope, 'twill not be long,
And we shall sing a sweeter song.

4 "Some day," we say, O Lord, how long
Must right succumb to boasting wrong?
"Some day"—sweet hope our souls endow,
Till we can feel 'tis almost now.

TIME TO SING.

D. R. LUCAS. Z. M. PARVIN.

3 Oh, sing when loneliness,
　　Enshrouds thy saddened heart,
　'Twill bring the Savior near,
　　And bid the gloom depart.

4 Oh, sing when death draws near,
　　To cheer the dying hour,
　'Twill lift the soul above
　　The tyrant's fearful power.

AGRIPPA AND PAUL.

D. R. LUCAS. Z. M. PARVIN.

1 A king sat on his throne of state, Before him, | bound with | chain,
  Appeared the captive Christian, Paul, Prepared for | death or | pain.
2 One standing there before the throne, The other | sitting | down,
  From calmness of his mien it seemed, The chained one | wore the | crown.
3 "I think myself, most happy king, That I be- | fore thee | may,
  Most freely speak of all the things The charges | on me | lay.
4 " For I am free from guilt, and tell The things both | seen and | heard,
  The resurrection of the dead, According | to the | Word.
5 " Agrippa, dost thou not believe What prophets | have fore- | told,
  Through all the ages of the past, These latter | days un- | fold?
6 " I know that thou believest well, For in the | light of | day,
  These things were not which thou hast heard, In corners | hid a- | way."
7 " Almost a Christian, Paul, I am Persuaded | now to | be."
  " Almost a Christian," Paul replied, " I would thou | wert like | me.
8 "And all that hear me speak this day, Were alto- | gether | free
  As I, except these bonds, and then, In love we | might a- | gree."

COME TO JESUS, JUST NOW.

Behold! now is the day of salvation.

2 He will save you.
3 Oh, believe him.
4 He is able.
5 He is willing.
6 He'll receive you.
7 Flee to Jesus,
8 Call unto him.
9 He will hear you.
10 He'll have mercy.
11 He'll forgive you.
12 He will cleanse you.
13 He'll renew you.
14 He will clothe you.
15 Jesus loves you.

74. CHRIST'S LOVE FOR THE CHURCH. C. M.

D. R. Lucas.   *Eph v: 25.*   Harmonized by Helen Walker.

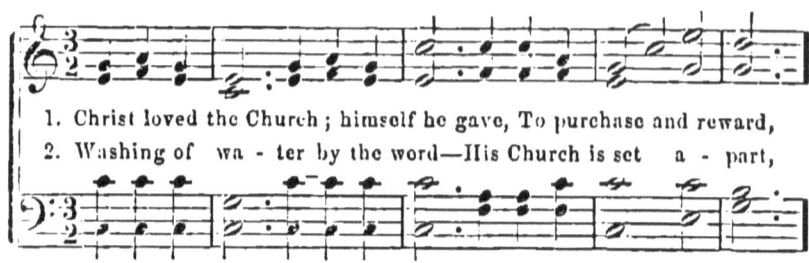

1. Christ loved the Church; himself he gave, To purchase and reward,
2. Washing of water by the word—His Church is set apart,

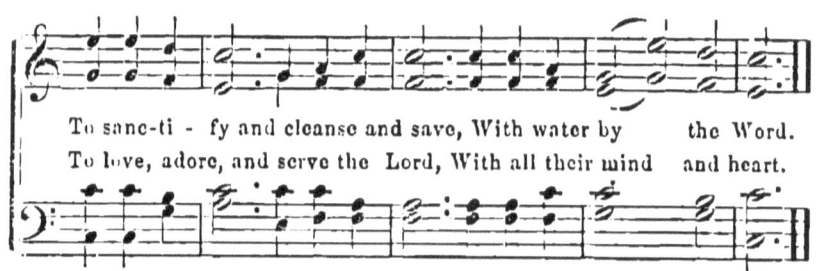

To sanc-ti-fy and cleanse and save, With water by the Word.
To love, adore, and serve the Lord, With all their mind and heart.

3 The Church he calls his own, his Bride,
His temple, and his flock,
His kingdom, vineyard, and his pride,
His house upon a rock.

4 The Church the body, Christ the head,
The bride he gave his name;
Oh, let her wide his glories spread,
His grace to all proclaim.

What shall I do with Jesus.—Matt. xxvii: 22.

1 What shall I do with Jesus, who
Is called God's holy Son?
Shall I believe, accept, and live?
Reject, and be undone?

2 I will believe him for his love,
And trust him for his grace;
I will believe, his mercy prove,
Make him my hiding-place.

3 I will confess his holy name,
Confess him every-where,
I will confess his every claim,
His power and love declare.

4 I will obey his great commands,
And heed his every call,
I will obey with heart and hands,
Give him my life, my all.
                D. R. Lucas.

Joy to the World.

1 Joy to the world! the Lord is come;
Let earth receive her King;
Let every heart prepare him room,
And heaven and nature sing.

2 Joy to the earth! the Savior reigns,
Let men their songs employ;
While fields and floods, rocks, hills, and plains,
Repeat the sounding joy.

3 No more let sins and sorrows grow,
Nor thorns infest the ground;
He comes to make his blessings flow
Far as the curse is found.

4 He rules the world with truth and grace,
And makes the nations prove
The glories of his righteousness,
And wonders of his love.
                Watts.

BALERMA. C. M.

D. R. Lucas.
Scottish.

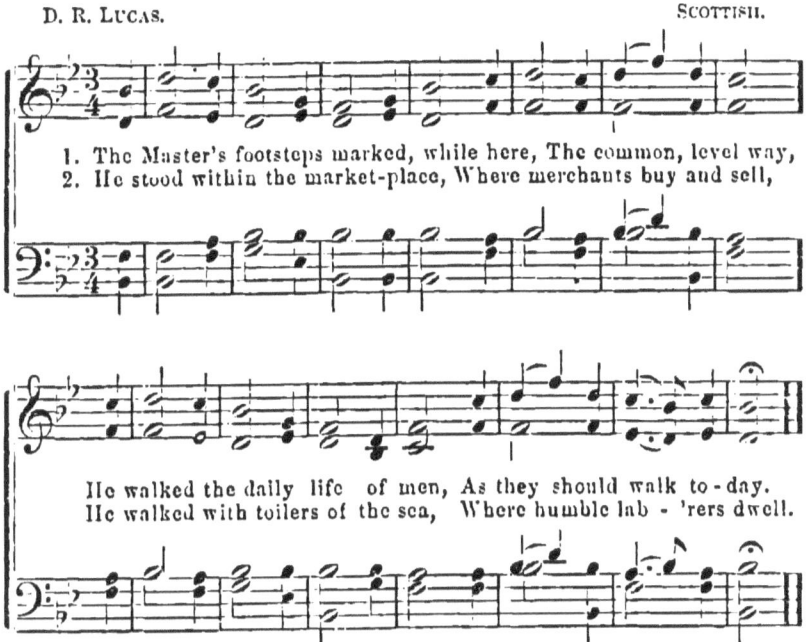

1. The Master's footsteps marked, while here, The common, level way,
  He walked the daily life of men, As they should walk to-day.
2. He stood within the market-place, Where merchants buy and sell,
  He walked with toilers of the sea, Where humble lab-'rers dwell.

3 He stood beside the cradled babe,
  At marriage feasts appeared,
When sickness laid its painful stroke,
  In death, the dying cheered.

4 Oh, let us all in every act,
  Of life while here below,
Take Christ with us in every work,
  That we his life may show.

Providence.

1 God notes the little sparrows fall,
  And shows his watchful care,
Then why should fear and doubt enthrall,
  Or sorrow bring despair?

2 God hears the ravens when they cry,
  Supplies them with their food,
And surely he to us is nigh,
  To love and do us good.

3 God knows and numbers every hair,
  That on our heads may grow,
And he will hear our humble prayer,
  Tho' words be weak and slow.

4 Oh, let these thoughts our hearts inspire,
  With proof that God is love,
Till all our fears of ill expire,
  Despair and doubt remove.

D. R. Lucas.

Aspirations.—2 Cor. v: 2.

1 We yearn for joys we can not see,
  We sigh for bliss to come,
The soul of man unconsciously,
  Looks upward for a home.

2 We know that matter can not take
  That which it did not give,
And tho' the rack our bodies break,
  Our spirits still must live.

3 The pain, the groan, the tear, the sigh,
  That mark the trembling frame,
Are but the souls deep, earnest cry,
  In its undying flame.

4 The whole creation groaning, taught
  That hope is not in vain,
For tho' subjected now, 'twill not
  Eternal thus remain.

D. R. Lucas.

SAFE WITHIN THE VEIL.*

E. ADAMS. J. M. EVANS.

1. "Land ahead!" its fruits are waving O'er the hills of fadeless green;
And the living waters laving Shores where heavenly forms are seen.

CHORUS.
Rocks and storms I'll fear no more, When on that e-ter-nal shore;
Drop the an-chor! furl the sail! I am safe with-in the vail!

2 Onward, bark! the cape I'm rounding,
See the blessed wave their hands;
Hear the harps of God resounding
From the bright immortal bands.

3 There, let go the anchor, riding
On this calm and silvery bay;
Seaward fast the tide is gliding,
Shores in sunlight stretch away.

4 Now we're safe from all temptation,
All the storms of life are past;
Praise the Rock of our salvation,
We are safe at home at last.

* From "Bright Jewels," by per. of Biglow & Main.

DENNIS. S. M. 77

FAWCETT. NAGELI.

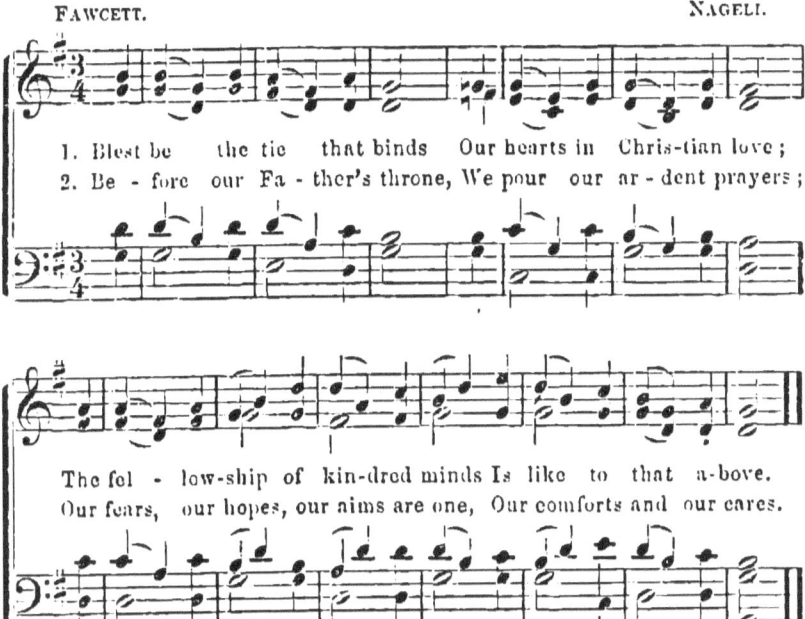

1. Blest be the tie that binds Our hearts in Christian love;
2. Before our Father's throne, We pour our ardent prayers;
The fellowship of kindred minds Is like to that above.
Our fears, our hopes, our aims are one, Our comforts and our cares.

3 We share our mutual woes,
  Our mutual burdens bear,
And often for each other flows
  The sympathizing tear.

4 When we asunder part,
  It gives us inward pain;
But we shall still be joined in heart,
  And hope to meet again.

The Heavenly Armor.—Eph. vi: 13.
Tune—"SAFE WITHIN THE VAIL."

1 Gird yourself with heavenly armor,
  In the conflict here with wrong,
Lift on high Messiah's banner,
  In the power of God be strong.

Chorus.—We will conquer all our foes,
  For our Savior leads the way,
After triumph comes repose,
  In the land of endless day.

2 Have your loins with truth encircled,
  Righteousness for breastplate wear,
On your feet put Gospel sandals,
  For the march and war prepare.

3 Take the shield of faith to guard you
  From the fiery darts you meet,
On your head salvation's helmet,
  Will your armor make complete.

4 Word of God, sword of the Spirit,
  As you go take in your hand:
Watch and pray, be true and faithful,
  And a victor you shall stand.
                D. R. LUCAS.

Shining Shore.

1 My days are gliding swiftly by,
  And I, a pilgrim stranger,
Would not detain them as they fly,
  Those hours of toil and danger.

Chorus.
For now we stand on Jordan's strand,
  Our friends are passing over;
And just before the shining shore,
  We may almost discover.

2 We'll gird our loins, my brethren dear,
  Our heavenly home discerning;
Our absent Lord has left us word,
  Let every lamp be burning.

3 Should coming days be cold and dark,
  We need not cease our singing;
That perfect rest naught can molest,
  Where golden harps are ringing.

4 Let sorrow's rudest tempest blow,
  Each cord on earth to sever,
Our King says come, and there's our
  Forever! oh, forever!   [home.
                NELSON.

HOME OF THE SOUL. Concluded.

2 Oh, that home of the soul in my visions and dreams,
  Its bright jasper walls I can see;
Till I fancy but thinly the vail intervenes
  :∥: Between the fair city and me.

3 That unchangeable home is for you and for me,
  Where Jesus of Nazareth stands;
The King of all kingdoms forever is he,
  :∥: And he holdeth our crowns in his hands. :∥:

4 Oh, how sweet it will be in that beautiful land,
  So free from all sorrow and pain:
With songs on our lips and with harps in our hands
  :∥: To meet one another again. :∥:

The Resurrection.—1 *Cor.* xv: 22.

1 As in Adam all die, so in Christ all shall live,
  But each in his order arise,
The good and the evil, and each one shall give
  His account to the judge in the skies.

2 All our bodies are sown in corruption on earth,
  In dishonor and weakness repose;
But in honor and glory they'll gain a new birth,
  And exult o'er the greatest of foes.

3 For one star from another doth difference show,
  In glory and honor on high,
And the God of all power, if he will can bestow
  A body that never can die.

4 So we'll sing our great hope of release from the grave,
  For the promise is made full and free,
That the Savior who conquered will rescue and save
  Those who sleep in the earth and the sea.
                                    D. R. LUCAS.

Joy unspeakable and full of glory.—1 *Peter* i: 8.

1 How happy are they who their Savior obey,
  And have laid up their treasures above!
Tongue can not express the sweet comfort and peace
  Of a soul in its earliest love!

2 This comfort is mine, since the favor divine
  I have found in the blood of the Lamb;
Since the truth I believed what a joy I've received,
  What a heaven in Jesus' blest name.

3 'Tis a heaven below my Redeemer to know,
  And the angels can do nothing more
Than to fall at his feet, and the story repeat,
  And the lover of sinners adore.

4 Now my remnant of days will I spend to his praise,
  Who has died me from sin to redeem;
Whether many or few, all my years are his due,
  They shall all be devoted to him.

5 What a mercy is this! what a heaven of bliss!
  How unspeakably happy am I,
Gathered into the fold, with believers enrolled—
  With believers to live and to die.   C. WESLEY.

I WILL SING FOR JESUS.

Making melody in your hearts to the Lord.

PHILIP PHILLIPS, by per.

1. I will sing for Jesus; With his blood he bought me,
And all a-long my pilgrim way His loving hand has brought me.
2. Can there o-ver-take me A-ny dark dis-as-ter,
While I sing for Je-sus, My bless-ed, blessed Mas-ter?

CHORUS.
Oh, help me sing for Je-sus, Help me tell the sto-ry,
Of him who did re-deem us, The Lord of life and glo-ry.

3 I will sing for Jesus!
His name alone prevailing,
Shall be my sweetest music,
When heart and flesh are failing.

4 Still I'll sing for Jesus!
Oh, how will I adore him,
Among the cloud of witnesses,
Who cast their crowns before him.

'TIS ALWAYS NEW.

For if, when we were enemies, we were reconciled to God by the death of his Son.
Rom. v: 10.

Mrs. Lydia Baxter. — Z. M. Parvin.

1. 'Tis always new, and thus we sing The same old Bible sto-ry,
2. Forever new those sweet old strains, The music and the num-ber;

Of Jesus' life and death to bring, Fresh rays of heavenly glo-ry;
That once, on fair Judea's plains, The shepherd's filled with wonder;
D. S. Of Jesus' life and death to show The way to heavenly glo - ry.

'Tis always new, this precious truth, He died for manhood, age, and youth.
We'll sing again that song of love, With angels 'round the throne above.

CHORUS.

'Tis always new, 'tis always new, This dear old Bi - ble sto - ry,

3 We gather round the cross and hear
That same old melting story;
It falls in mercy on the ear,
And fills the soul with glory;
Oh, gracious Savior can it be,
Thy precious blood was shed for me?

4 O blessed Jesus, when above,
The golden harps are given,
For evermore new songs of love
Shall fill the courts of heaven!
Oh, may we there our Savior meet,
And join that song divinely sweet.

GO, WORK FOR JESUS.

The harvest truly is plenteous, but the laborers are few.—Matt. ix: 37.

MISS M. G. DANFORTH.   Z. M. PARVIN.

1. Be-hold, the field is white, I hear The Lord of har-vest say,
Dis-ci-ple, hearest thou the call? Go, work for me to-day.

CHORUS.
Behold, the harvest field is white, The la-bor-ers how few, how few;
For all who wish to serve the Lord, There's work enough to do.

2 Why stand ye idle all the day,
Its hours are flying fast,
Its golden moments can not be
Redeemed from out the past.

3 Then work for Jesus day by day,
The golden sheaves bring in,
The blessed Master then will say
To you the glad "well done."

Over There. 8s and 9s.

1 Oh, think of a home over there
  By the side of the river of light,
Where the saints all immortal and fair,
  Are robed in their garments of white,
    Over there, over there,
  Oh, think of the home over there.

Cho.—Over there, over there, over there,
  Oh, think of a home over there.

2 Oh, think of the friends over there,
  Who before us the journey have trod,
Of the songs that they breathe on the air,
  In their home in the palace of God,
    Over there, over there,
  Oh, think of the friends over there.

3 My Savior is now over there.
  There my kindred and friends are at rest,
Then away from my sorrow and care,
  Let me fly to the land of the blest,
    Over there, over there,
  My Savior is now over there.

4 I'll soon be at home over there,
  For the end of my journey I see;
Many dear to my heart over there,
  Are watching and waiting for me,
    Over there, over there,
  I'll soon be at home over there.
                T. C. O'KANE.

Watch. S. M.

1 My soul be on thy guard;
  Ten thousand foes arise;
The hosts of sin are pressing hard
  To draw thee from the skies.

2 Oh, watch, and fight, and pray,
  The battle ne'er give o'er;
Renew it boldly every day,
  And help divine implore.

3 Ne'er think the victory won,
  Nor lay thine armor down:
Thy arduous work will not be done
  Till thou obtain thy crown.

4 Fight on my soul, till death
  Shall bring thee to thy God;
He'll take thee at thy parting breath,
  To his divine abode.
                HEATH.

Tarry with Me. 8s and 7s.

1 Tarry with me, O my Savior,
  For the day is passing by;
See, the shades of evening gather,
  And the night is drawing nigh.

Cho.—Tarry with me blessed Jesus,
  Leave me not till morning light,
For I'm lonely here without thee—
  Tarry with me through the night.

2 Many friends were gathered round me
  In the bright days of the past,
But the grave has closed above them,
  And I linger here at last.

3 Deeper, deeper grow the shadows;
  Paler now the glowing west;
Swift the night of death advances—
  Shall it be the night of rest?

4 Tarry with me, O my Savior!
  Lay my head upon thy breast
Till the morning; then awake me—
  Morning of eternal rest!

Hark! ten thousand Harps. 8s and 7s —*peculiar.*

1 Hark! ten thousand harps and voices
  Sound the note of praise above;
Jesus reigns and heav'en rejoices;
  Jesus reigns, the God of love:
See, he sits on yonder throne;
Jesus rules the world alone.

2 Jesus, hail! whose glory brightens
  All above and gives it worth;
Lord of life, thy smile enlightens,
  Cheers and charms thy saints on earth:
When we think of love like thine,
Lord, we own it love divine.

3 King of glory, reign forever!
  Thine an everlasting crown;
Nothing from thy love shall sever
  Those whom thou hast made thine own;
Happy objects of thy grace,
Destined to behold thy face.

4 Savior, hasten thine appearing;
  Bring, O bring the glorious day,
When the awful summons hearing,
  Heav'n and earth shall pass away:
Then, with golden harps we'll sing,
"Glory, glory to our King!"
                KELLY.

WORK AND REST.

D. R. Lucas.   Dr. W. Lucas, 1820.

1. Our life is here a life of toil, Of sorrow and unrest, We labor oft for perfect peace, Yet ne'er are fully blest, Yet ne'er are fully blest;

2 Hope paints the clouds with silver threads,
But still the clouds remain,
Their angry frowns above our heads,
Oft reappear again.

3 It must be death will ope the gates,
The portal into life,
Where peace will be th' eternal state,
And rest succeed the strife.

4 Then let us toil, 'twill soon be o'er,
Let labor come to-day,
The rest from work is just before
The rest that lasts for aye.

Come let us anew.

1 Come let us anew
Our journey pursue—
Roll round with the year,
And never stand still till the Master
His adorable will   [appear;
Let us gladly fulfill,
And our talents improve   [of love.
By the patience of hope, and the labor

2 Our life is a dream;
Our time, as a stream,
Glides swiftly away,   [stay;
And the fugitive moment refuses to
The arrow is flown;
The moment is gone;
The millennial year   [near.
Rushes on to our view, and eternity's

3 Oh, that each, in the day
Of his coming, may say
"I have fought my way thro';
I have finished the work thou didst
give me to do;"
Oh, that each from his Lord,
May receive the glad word,
"Well and faithfully done;
Enter into my joy, and sit down on
my throne."   C. Wesley.

CITY OF GOD. Concluded. 87

To be there, to be there, Dear Redeemer, we long to be there.

2 There their sorrows and trials are o'er,
 With the Savior eternally blest,
There the wicked annoy them no more,
 There the weary forever find rest.

3 There the songs of immortals are heard,
 Thro' all the bright portals of bliss,
Nor is sickness or death to be feared,
 In a region so glorious as this.

4 There shall friendships begun here below,
 That by death have been ruthlessly riven,
Be renewed, for we surely shall know
 All our friends when we meet them in heaven.

5 With the angels and glorified saints,
 In the city of glory to be,
As for waters the wounded hart pants,
 So, Jerus'lem, we're panting for thee.

Land of Promise.

1 There is a land of pure delight,
 Where saints immortal reign,
Infinite day excludes the night,
 And pleasures banish pain.

2 There, everlasting spring abides
 And never-withering flowers,
Death, like a narrow sea, divides
 This heavenly land from ours.

3 Sweet fields, beyond the swelling flood,
 Stand dressed in living green;
So to the Jews old Canaan stood,
 While Jordan rolled between.

4 But tim'rous mortals start and shrink,
 To cross this narrow sea;
And linger, shivering on the brink,
 And fear to launch away.
   WATTS.

The dear sweet Bells of Memory.

1 Sweet mem'ry bells! their witching chimes,
Have charms as dear as olden rhymes;
We hear them oft at twilight hour
When sets the sun and shuts the flow'r.

2 When Luna's mystic silver light
Bathes hill and dale at noon or night,
Then voices ring with magic strain,
Breaking the calm with sweet refrain.

3 Telling of childhood's joyous lays,
And hopes and fears of by-gone days;
Of bridal vows and farewells said,
And solemn dirges for the dead.

4 Soon, soon our weary feet shall tread
That land where no sad tears are shed;
Soon we shall clasp the hand of friends,
Where with the song no discord blends.
   SCRAP BOOK.

88. OH, WHAT MUST IT BE TO BE THERE?

From the "Amethyst."   A. L. KLAR.

1. We speak of the realms of the blest, That country so bright and so fair, And oft are its glories confessed, But what must it be to be there?
2. We speak of its pathways of gold, Of its walls decked with jewels so rare, Of its wonders and pleasures untold, But what must it be to be there?
3. We speak of its freedom from sin, From sorrow, temptation, and care, From trials without and within, But what must it be to be there?

CHORUS.

Oh, what must it be to be there, to be there? Oh, what must it be to be there, to be there? The home of the soul, the place of the blest, Oh, what must it be to be there?

BE UP AND BE DOING. Concluded. 91

Be up and be do-ing, be up and be doing, Work while it is day.

TALLULA. C. M.

D. R. LUCAS.   FRANK M. DAVIS.

1. This is re - lig - ion, pure and full, Of heaven-ly hope and joy, Un - spot - ted from the world to live, In mer - cy's sweet em - ploy.
2. The sweet - est com - fort to the heart, As day draws to its close, Is know-ing of some ef - fort made, To light - en hu - man woes.
3. To know each day the Lord was near, In those who suf - fer pain, That wid - ow's cry and or - phan's tear, Have not ap - pealed in vain.
4. That deeds of kind - ness, mer - cy, love, Have been our con - stant care, Our souls with - in us burn to feel How sweet a cross we bear.

HEAVENLY MANSIONS.

Melody and Words by L. H. JAMESON. Har. by Z. M. PARVIN.

1. There are man-sions pre-pared in the skies, By the Sav-ior who passed on be-fore, And the Chris-tian, whenev-er he dies, Finds a home where the saints die no more.

2. There the "Lamb that was slain" ev-er lives, In the light of the glo-ry of God, And to all that o-bey him he gives Robes made white in his own pre-cious blood.

CHORUS.
Die no more, die no more, Die no more, die no more, Finds a home where the saints die no more, die no more, die no more, die no more

HEAVENLY MANSIONS. Concluded.

die no more, die no more, Finds a home where the saints die no more.

3 There the Father of mercy abides,
  Whom the saints and the angels adore,
And the river of life gently glides
  From his throne in that world evermore.

4 There the saints walk with Jesus in white,
  They are burdened with sorrows no more,
But are filled with ecstatic delight,
  In their home on that bright, balmy shore.

5 There are mansions prepared for us all,
  And the Savior is calling us home;
Sinners, hearken! the Bride joins the call,
  Come to-day, for the Spirit says, Come.

OLD HUNDRED. L. M.

D. R. LUCAS.   Jude i: 24.

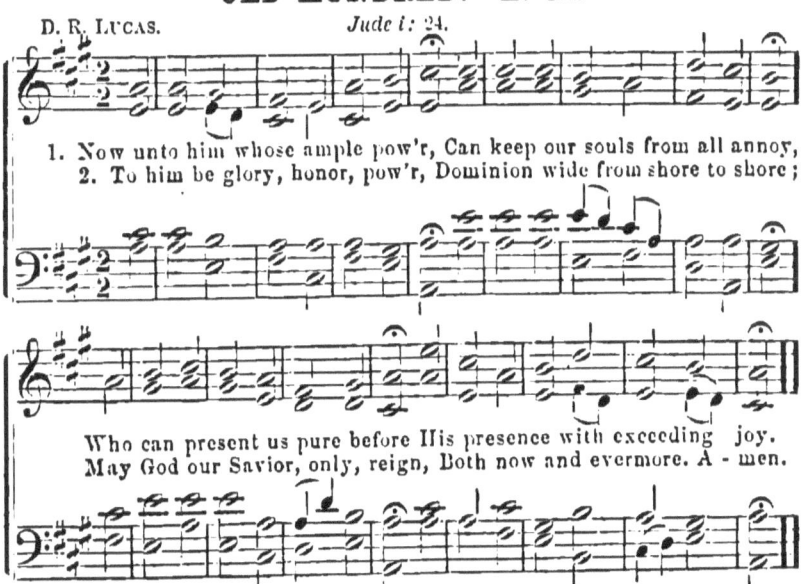

1. Now unto him whose ample pow'r, Can keep our souls from all annoy,
2. To him be glory, honor, pow'r, Dominion wide from shore to shore;

Who can present us pure before His presence with exceeding joy.
May God our Savior, only, reign, Both now and evermore. A - men.

Let all the people praise thee.

1 From all that dwell below the skies,
Let the Creator's praise arise;
Let the Redeemer's name be sung
Thro' every land, by every tongue.

2 Eternal are thy mercies, Lord;
Eternal truth attends thy word; [shore,
Thy praise shall sound from shore to
Till suns shall rise and set no more.

EVENING SONG.

Melody and Words by L. H. JAMESON. Har. by Z. M. PARVIN.

1. Our Father in heaven, In mercy now hear us,
As shadows of even Are gathering o'er us,
Grant thou to be near us, Thro'out the dark night,
To keep and to cheer us Till morning's clear light.

2. May bright guardian angels Encircle the beds,
To soften the pillows Where rest weary heads,
May sweet cheering visions In mercy be given,
Of loved ones and lost ones, Long since gone to heaven. A-men.

3 Thus far thou hast led us,
And guarded our way,
Thy bounty has fed us
From day unto day;
When trouble and sorrow
Endured for the night,
The incoming morrow
Brought joy with its light.

4 Forgive us the errors
Committed to-day,
And grant us protection,
We earnestly pray;
In Jesus' blest name,
Thy grace we implore,
And thine be the glory,
Henceforth, evermore.

APOSTOLIC HYMNS AND SONGS.

Christ our Confidence. 6s and 4s.

1 My faith looks up to thee,
  Thou Lamb of Calvary:
    Savior divine;
  Now hear me while I pray;
  Take all my guilt away;
  O, let me, from this day,
    Be wholly thine.

2 May thy rich grace impart
  Strength to my fainting heart;
    My zeal inspire;
  As thou hast died for me,
  O, may my love to thee
  Pure, warm, and changeless be—
    A living fire.

3 While life's dark maze I tread,
  And griefs around me spread,
    Be thou my guide;
  Bid darkness turn to day,
  Wipe sorrow's tears away,
  Nor let me ever stray
    From thee aside.

4 When ends life's transient dream,
  When death's cold, sullen stream
    Shall o'er me roll;
  Blest Savior, then, in love,
  Fear and distress remove;
  O bear me safe above—
    A ransomed soul.
            RAY PALMER.

Invitation to Praise.

1 O for a thousand tongues to sing
  My great Redeemer's praise;
  The glories of my God and King,
  The triumphs of his grace.

2 My gracious Master, and my God,
  Assist me to proclaim,—
  To spread through all the earth abroad,
  The honors of thy Name.

3 Jesus!—the Name that charms our fears,
  That bids our sorrows cease:
  'Tis music in the sinner's ears,
  'Tis life, and health and peace.

4 He breaks the power of cancelled sin,
  He sets the pris'ner free;
  His blood can make the foulest clean;
  His blood avail'd for me.
            C. WESLEY.

Jesus, Lover of my Soul.

1 Jesus, lover of my soul,
    Let me to thy bosom fly,
  While the billows near me roll,
    While the tempest still is high;
  Hide me, O my Savior, hide,
    Till the storm of life is past;
  Safe into the haven guide,
    O receive my soul at last.

2 Other refuge have I none,
    Hangs my helpless soul on thee!
  Leave, O leave me not alone,
    Still support and comfort me:
  All my trust on thee is stay'd,
    All my help from thee I bring,
  Cover my defenseless head
    With the shadow of thy wing.

3 Thou, O Christ, art all I want,
    Boundless love in thee I find;
  Raise the fallen, cheer the faint,
    Heal the sick and lead the blind;
  Just and holy is thy name,
    Prince of Peace and Righteousness;
  Most unworthy, Lord, I am,
    Thou art full of love and grace.

4 Plenteous grace with thee is found,
    Grace to pardon all my sin;
  Let the healing streams abound,
    Make and keep me pure within:
  Thou of life the fountain art,
    Freely let me take of thee;
  Spring thou up within my heart,
    Rise to all eternity. C. WESLEY.

Faith in Christ.

1 How sweet the name of Jesus sounds
    In a believer's ear;
  It soothes his sorrows, heals his
      wounds,
    And drives away his fear.
  Cho.—I do believe, I now believe,
    That Jesus died for me;
  And through his blood, his prec-
      ious blood,
    I shall from sin be free.

2 It makes the wounded spirit whole,
    And calms the troubled breast;
  'Tis manna to the hungry soul,
    And to the weary rest.

3 Weak is the effort of my heart,
    And cold my warmest thought;
  But when I see thee as thou art,
    I'll praise thee as I ought.

4 Till then I would thy love proclaim
    With every fleeting breath;
  And may the music of thy name
    Refresh my soul in death.
            NEWTON.

Temperance Victory.

Tune—"BY AND BY."

1 For the honor of our God,
  For the safety of our land,
 We are fighting for our homes,
  We're an earnest temp'rance band.
Cho.—By and by, by and by,
  We shall all from rum be free,
 By and by, by and by,
  We shall gain the victory.

2 We have put our armor on,
  And will fight the monster sin,
 Never lay our weapons down,
  Till the victory we win.

3 'Tis a glorious conflict now,
  Worthy all our best desires,
 And within our trusting souls,
  Every hopeful thought inspires.
      R. D. LUCAS.

Father, I have Sinned.—Luke xv. 18.

1 Love for all! and can it be?
  Can I hope it is for me?
 I, who strayed so long ago,
  Strayed so far, and fell so low!

2 I, the disobedient child,
  Wayward, passionate, and wild;
 I, who left my Father's home
  In forbidden ways to roam!

3 I, who spurned his loving hold,
  I, who would not be controlled;
 I, who would not hear his call,
  I, the willful prodigal!

4 I, who wasted and misspent
  Every talent he had lent;
 I, who sinned again, again,
  Giving every passion rein!

5 To my Father can I go?—
  At his feet myself I'll throw,
 In his house there yet may be
  Place, a servant's place, for me.

6 See, my Father waiting stands;
  See, he reaches out his hands;
 God is love! I know, I see,
  Love for me—yes, even me.
      LONGFELLOW.

Heaven is my Home. 6s and 4s.

1 I'm but a stranger here;
   Heaven is my home;
  Earth is a desert drear;
   Heaven is my home.
  Danger and sorrow stand
  Round me on every hand,
  Heaven is my fatherland—
   Heaven is my home.

2 What though the tempests rage,
   Heaven is my home:
  Short is my pilgrimage;
   Heaven is my home.
  And Time's wild wintry blast
  Soon will be overpast.
  I shall reach home at last;
   Heaven is my home.

3 There at my Savior's side,
   Heaven is my home;
  I shall be glorified;
   Heaven is my home.
  There, with the good and blest,
  Those I loved most and best,
  I shall for ever rest;
   Heaven is my home.

4 Therefore I'll murmur not;
   Heaven is my home;
  Whate'er my earthly lot,
   Heaven is my home.
  For I shall surely stand,
  There at my Lord's right hand,
  Heaven is my fatherland—
   Heaven is my home.
      T. R. TAYLOR.

To-day. 6s and 4s.

1 To-day the Savior calls:
   Ye wand'rers, come:
  O, ye benighted souls,
   Why longer roam?

2 To-day the Savior calls;
   O, hear him now;
  Within these sacred walls
   To Jesus bow.

3 To-day the Savior calls;
   For refuge fly;
  The storm of vengeance falls,
   And death is nigh.

4 The Spirit calls to-day;
   Yield to his power;
  O, grieve him not away;
   'Tis mercy's hour.

APOSTOLIC HYMNS AND SONGS.

"Touch it not."

Tune—"THERE IS LIGHT."

1. If you would not be a drunkard,
You must never touch a drop
Of the wine that looks so tempting
In the sparkling, ruby cup.

Cho.—I will never touch the cup,
I will never drink a drop;
If the tempter comes to me,
I shall from his pow'r be free.

2 It is such a small beginning,
Tho' it innocent may seem,
That will lead you into sinning,
And the drunkard's horrid dream.

3 Every kind of beer and cider,
That the drinker first will use,
If you would not be a drunkard,
You must always firmly refuse.

4 If you would not lose your reason,
And become a helpless sot,
You can only find your safety
In the motto—"Touch it not."
D. R. LUCAS.

Crusaders' Battle Hymn.

Tune—"GLORY HALLELUJAH." Key of B♭.

1 The light of truth is breaking,
On the mountain tops it gleams,
Let it flash along our valleys,
Let it glitter on our streams,
Till all our land awakens,
In its flush of golden beams—
Our God is marching on.

Cho.—Glory, glory, hallelujah,
Glory, glory, hallelujah,
Glory, glory, hallelujah,
Our God is marching on.

2 From morning's early watches,
Till the setting of the sun,
We will never flag or falter
In the work we have begun,
Till the forts have all surrendered,
And the victory is won.—
The time is marching on.

3 We wield no carnal weapons,
And we hurl no fiery dart,
But with words of love and reason,
We are sure to win the heart,
And persuade the poor transgressor
To prefer the better part,—
Our God is marching on.

Battle Hymn of the Crusaders. Key of B♭.

1 "Mine eyes have seen the glory
Of the coming of the Lord,"
The fulfillment of his promise,
As recorded in his Word;
And the smiting of the wicked
With his "terrible swift sword,"
When God is marching on.

Cho.—Glory, glory, hallelujah!
Glory, glory, hallelujah!
Glory, glory, hallelujah!
Our God is marching on!

2 The woes of drunkenness on earth
Have mounted up to heaven,
The wrongs to parents, children, wives,
Are known and unforgiven,
And long God's light and truth in vain
With guilty men have striven;
Now God is marching on.

3 The sinner hears the voice of God
Now sounding in his ears,
It mingleth with kind women's voice,
In songs, and prayers, and tears,
And fills his heart with sense of guilt,
And penitence and fears;
God's truth *is* marching on.

4 Let all God's people lift their hearts,
And from the mountain's top,
And from the plains and valleys deep,
Send up a joyful shout,
The Lord is God, and from the earth
This curse he will blot out;
For God is marching on.

PRESSING ONWARD.

Words and Music by Geo. H. Spring.

1. We're hast'ning at our King's command, A journey to pursue,
2. Earth has no portion, rest, or joy, To fill our vast desire,
3. We seek a city out of sight, Jerusalem above,
4. We'll bless our King from day to day, His goodness we'll adore,
5. Tho' foes oppose, with singing still, To Zion we will go,

We're going to the promised land, Our heritage to view.
To nobler, purer bliss on high, Our longing souls aspire.
Where throned in heavenly splendor bright, Abides the God we love.
Who opened us the heavenly way, By passing on before.
For God will guard us on until Our journey's end we know.

CHORUS:

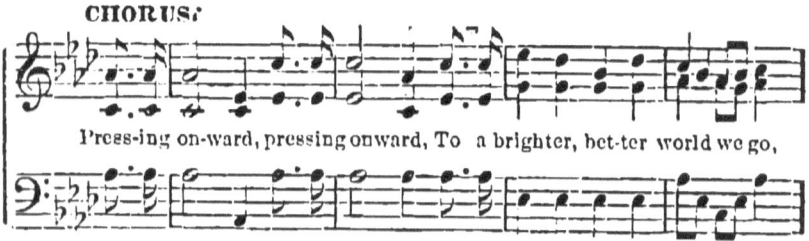

Pressing onward, pressing onward, To a brighter, better world we go,

Pressing onward, pressing onward, Ever nearing heaven, our home

*From "Pearly Gates."

Temperance Song.
Tune—"Pressing Onward."

1 We're marching on to victory,
   We're soldiers true and tried,
   We'll sing at last with loud huzza,
   A triumph far and wide.
Cho.—We shall conquer, we shall con-
    quer,
   We will drive our foe to sure
    defeat;
   On to vict'ry, on to vict'ry,
   We will never sound retreat.

2 We wage our war upon the cup,
   That sparkles red with wine,
   And in its place forevermore,
   Shall pure cold water reign.

3 To lift the fallen, cheer the faint,
   Our mission still shall be,
   And never cease till all mankind
   From rum's sad fate are free.
                P. H. Bristow.

Our Souls are in the Savior's Hand.
C. M.

1 Our souls are in the Savior's hand,
   And he will keep them still,
   And you and I shall surely stand
   With him on Zion's hill.

2 Him eye to eye we there shall see,
   Our face like his shall shine;
   O! what a glorious company,
   When saints and angels join!

3 O! what a joyful meeting there,
   In robes of white array!
   Palms in our hands we all shall bear,
   And crowns that ne'er decay!

4 When we've been there ten thousand
    years,
   Bright shining as the sun,
   We've no less days to sing God's praise,
   Than when we first begun!

5 Then let us hasten to the day
   When all shall be brought home;
   Come, O Redeemer! come away!
   O Jesus! quickly come!

Our Land. C. M.

1 Lord, while for all mankind we pray,
   Of ev'ry clime and coast,
   O hear us for our native land—
   The land we love the most.

2 O guard our shores from ev'ry foe,
   With peace our borders bless,
   With prosp'rous times our cities crown.
   Our fields with plenteousness.

3 Unite us in the sacred love
   Of knowledge, truth, and thee;
   And let our hills and valleys shout
   The songs of liberty.

4 Lord of the nations, thus to thee
   Our country we commend;
   Be thou her refuge and her trust,
   Her everlasting friend.
                Welford.

The Morning Cometh.—Isa. xxi. 12.
C. M.

1 Light of the lonely pilgrim's heart,
   Star of the coming day!
   Arise, and with thy morning beams
   Chase all our griefs away!

2 Come, blessed Lord! let every shore
   And answering island sing
   The praises of thy royal name,
   And own thee as their King.

3 Bid the whole earth responsive now
   To the bright world above,
   Break forth in sweetest strains of joy
   In memory of thy love.

4 Jesus! thy fair creation groans,
   The air, the earth, the sea,
   In unison with all our hearts,
   And calls aloud for thee.

5 Thine was the cross, with all its fruits
   Of grace and peace divine;
   Be thine the crown of glory now,
   The palm of victory thine!

Go to thy Rest, fair Child. S. M.

1 Go to thy rest, fair child!
   Go to thy dreamless bed,
While yet so gentle, undefiled,
   With blessing on thy head.

2 Fresh roses in thy hand,
   Buds on thy pillow laid,
Haste from this dark and fearful land
   Where flowers so quickly fade.

3 Before thy heart had learned
   In waywardness to stray;
Before thy feet had ever turned
   The dark and downward way;

4 Ere sin had seared the breast,
   Or sorrow woke the tear;
Rise to thy throne of changeless rest,
   In yon celestial sphere!

5 Because thy smile was fair,
   Thy lip and eye so bright,
Because thy loving cradle care
   Was such a dear delight;

6 Shall love, with weak embrace,
   Thy upward wing detain?
No! gentle angel, seek thy place
   Amid the cherub train.

"A Light unto my Path."—Psalm cxix.
105. C. M.

1 What glory gilds the sacred page,
   Majestic like the sun!
It gives a light to every age—
   It gives but borrows none.

2 The hand that gave it still supplies
   His gracious light and heat;
His truths upon the nations rise—
   They rise, but never set.

3 Let everlasting thanks be thine
   For such a bright display,
As makes the world of darkness shine
   With beams of heav'nly day.

4 My soul rejoices to pursue
   The paths of truth and love,
Till glory breaks upon my view
   In brighter worlds above.
             COWPER.

Mary at the Tomb. 7s Double.

1 Mary to the Savior's tomb
   Hasted at the early dawn;
Spice she brought, and sweet perfume,
   But the Lord she loved had gone.
For a while she lingering stood,
   Filled with sorrow and surprise;
Trembling while a crystal flood
   Issued from her weeping eyes.

2 Jesus, who is always near,
   Though too often unperceived,
Came, her drooping heart to cheer,
   Kindly asking why she grieved.
Though at first she knew him not,
   When he called her by her name,
She her heavy griefs forgot,
   For she found him still the same.

3 And her sorrows quickly fled,
   When she heard his welcome voice;
Christ had risen from the dead,
   Now he bids her heart rejoice:
What a change his word can make,
   Turning darkness into day;
You who weep for Jesus' sake,
   He will wipe your tears away.
             NEWTON.

C. M.

1 Thou art the Way—to thee alone
   From sin and death we flee;
And he who would the Father seek,
   Must seek him, Lord, by thee.

2 Thou art the Truth—thy word alone
   True wisdom can impart;
Thou only canst inform the mind,
   And purify the heart.

3 Thou art the Life—the rending tomb
   Proclaims thy conq'ring arm;
And those who put their trust in thee,
   Nor death nor hell shall harm.

4 Thou art the Way, the Truth, the Life;
   Grant us that way to know,
That truth to keep, that life to win,
   Whose joys eternal flow.
             DOANE.

Come, Sing to Me of Heaven. S. M.

1 Come, sing to me of heaven,
　　When I'm about to die;
　Sing songs of holy ecstasy,
　　To waft my soul on high.
Cho.—There'll be no sorrow there,
　　There'll be no sorrow there,
　In heaven above, where all is love,
　　There'll be no sorrow there.

2 When the last moment comes,
　　O, watch my dying face,
　To catch the bright seraphic glow,
　　Which on each feature plays.

3 Then to my raptured ear
　　Let one sweet song be given;
　Let music charm me last on earth,
　　And meet me first in heaven!

Sweet Hour of Prayer.

1 Sweet hour of prayer! sweet hour of prayer!
　That calls me from a world of care,
　And bids me at my Father's throne
　Make all my wants and wishes known:
　In seasons of distress and grief,
　My soul has often found relief,
　And oft escaped the tempter's snare,
　By thy return, sweet hour of prayer.

2 Sweet hour of prayer! sweet hour of prayer!
　Thy wings shall my petition bear,
　To him whose truth and faithfulness,
　Engage the waiting soul to bless;
　And since he bids me seek his face,
　Believe his word, and trust his grace,
　I'll cast on him my ev'ry care,
　And wait for thee, sweet hour of prayer!

Tune—"St. Thomas." S. M.

1 Let party names no more
　　The Christian world o'erspread;
　Gentile and Jew, and bond and free,
　　Are one in Christ their Head.

2 Among the saints on earth,
　　Let mutual love be found;
　Heirs of the same inheritance,
　　With mutual blessings crown'd.

3 Thus will the church below
　　Resemble that above,
　Where streams of pleasure ever flow,
　　And ev'ry heart is love.
　　　　　　　　　　Toplady.

Shall We Know?

1 When we hear the music ringing,
　　In the bright celestial dome,
　When sweet angel voices singing,
　　Gladly bid us welcome home
　To the land of ancient story,
　　Where the spirit knows no care,
　In that land of light and glory,
　　Shall we know each other there?

2 When the holy angels meet us,
　　As we go to join their band,
　Shall we know the friends that greet us
　　In that glorious spirit land?
　Shall we see the same eyes shining
　　On us as in days of yore?
　Shall we feel their dear arms twining,
　　Fondly round us as before?

3 Oh, ye weary, sad, and tossed ones,
　　Droop not, faint not by the way;
　You shall join the loved and just ones
　　In the land of perfect day,
　Harp-strings, touched by angel fingers,
　　Murmured in my raptured ear—
　Evermore their sweet song lingers—
　　We shall know each other there.

Funeral Hymn.

Tune—"Preach Christ."

1 Gone to the unseen home,
　　Home of the spirits blest,
　Gone where the pure rejoice,
　　And where the weary rest;
　Gone to the blissful land,
　　Gone with the loved and lost,
　Gone where the struggling souls
　　No more are tempest toss'd.

2 Gone to the spirit land,
　　Gone where the angels sing,
　Gone where no thoughts of woe,
　　Or pain will sorrow bring,
　Gone to the land of crowns,
　　Where cares no more annoy,
　Gone where the Savior's love
　　Fills every cup with joy.

3 Safe in the arms of Love,
　　Safe in the blessed light,
　Safe in the world of day,
　　A world that knows no night;
　Safe with the glorious host,
　　Safe on the other shore,
　Safe where the songs of love
　　Are heard forevermore.
　　　　　　　　D. R. Lucas.

Blessed they that Hunger. Matt. v. 6. S. M.

1 Hungry, and faint, and poor,
　　Behold us, Lord, again
　Assembled at thy mercy's door,
　　Thy bounty to obtain.

2 Thy word invites us nigh,
　　Or we would starve indeed;
　For we no money have to buy,
　　Nor righteousness to plead.

3. The food our spirits want,
　　Thy hand alone can give;
　O! hear the prayer of faith, and grant
　　That we may eat and live!

106. I AM WAITING.*

"All the days of my appointed time will I wait, till my change come."—Job xiv. 14.

Rev. Elisha A. Hoffman.   Frank M. Davis.

1. I am wait-ing for the summons That shall bid me turn my feet,
2. I am wait-ing till the an-gels Shall with flaming wings come down,
3. I am wait-ing, yet in pa-tience, Till my work is ful-ly done,

To the cit-y of Im-man - uel, There to walk the gold-en street.
To es-cort me to yon cit - y, There to wear the gold-en crown.
Ere my soul shall reach the mansions, Where the glo-ry is be - gun.

CHORUS.

I am wait - ing, calm-ly wait - ing, Till my Lord shall bid me come,

To a home with-in the mansions Of the new Je-ru-sa-lem.

*From "Gospel Echoes."

Lonely Waiting. 7s.

1 Years have come and passed away,
Golden locks have turned to gray,
Golden ringlets once so fair
Time has changed to silvery hair;
Yes, I've neared the river-side;
Soon I'll launch upon its tide;
Soon my boat with noiseless oar,
Safe will reach to yonder shore.

Cho.—Bring my harp to me again,
Let me sing some gentle strain;
Let me hear its chords once more,
Ere I pass to yon bright shore.

2 O, those chords with magic power
Take me back to childhood's hour,
To that cot beside the sea,
Where I knelt at mother's knee;
But that mother, she is gone—
Calm she sleeps beneath the stone;
While I wander here alone,
Sighing for a better home.

3 Soon I'll be among the blest,
Where the weary are at rest;
Soon I'll tread the golden shore,
Singing praises evermore :
Yes, my boat is on the stream—
I can see its waters gleam;
Soon I'll be where angels roam;
Dear old harp, I'm going home!

"Quit you like men, be strong."—1 Cor.
xvi. 13. 8s and 7s.

1 We are living, we are dwelling
In a grand and awful time,
In an age on ages telling,
To be living is sublime.

2 Hark! the onset! will ye fold your
Faith-clad arms in lazy lock?
Up, O up! ye drowsy soldier;
Worlds are charging to the shock:

3 Worlds are charging, heaven beholding!
Thou hast but an hour to fight;
Now the blazoned cross unfolding,
On! right onward for the right.

4 On! let all the soul within you
For the truth's sake go abroad;
Strike! let every nerve and sinew
Tell on ages—tell for God.
A. CONE.

Redeeming Love. 7s.

1 Now begin the heavenly theme;
Sing aloud in Jesus' name;
Ye who his salvation prove,
Triumph in redeeming love.

2 Ye who see the Father's grace
Beaming in the Savior's face,
As to Canaan on ye move,
Praise and bless redeeming love.

3 Mourning souls, dry up your tears
Banish all your guilty fear;
See your guilt and curse remove,
Canceled by redeeming love.

4 Welcome, all by sin oppressed,
Welcome to his sacred rest;
Nothing brought him from above,
Nothing but redeeming love.

5 Hither, then, your music bring;
Strike aloud each cheerful string;
Mortals, join the host above—
Join to praise redeeming love.
LANGFORD.

Thy judgments are a great deep. Psalm
xxxvi. 6. C. M.

1 God moves in a mysterious way
His wonders to perform;
He plants his footsteps in the sea,
And rides upon the storm.

2 Deep in unfathomable mines
Of never-failing skill,
He treasures up his bright designs,
And works his gracious will.

3 You fearful saints, fresh courage take,
The clouds you so much dread
Are big with mercy, and shall break,
In blessings on your head.

4 Judge not the Lord by feeble sense,
But trust him for his grace;
Behind a frowning providence
He hides a smiling face.

5 His purposes will ripen fast,
Unfolding every hour;
The bud may have a bitter taste,
But sweet will be the flower.

6 Blind unbelief is sure to err,
And scan his work in vain;
God is his own interpreter,
And he will make it plain.
COWPER.

I would not live alway. Job vii. 16. 11s.

1 I would not live alway; I ask not to stay,
  Where storm after storm rises dark o'er the way;
  The few cloudy mornings that dawn on us here,
  Are enough for life's woes, full enough for its cheer.

2 I would not live alway: no, welcome the tomb;
  Since Jesus has lain there, I dread not its gloom;
  There sweet be my rest, till he bid me arise
  To hail him in triumph descending the skies.

3 Who, who would live alway, away from his God,
  Away from yon heaven, that blissful abode,
  Where the rivers of pleasure flow o'er the bright plains,
  And the noontide of glory eternally reigns;

4 Where the saints of all ages in harmony meet,
  Their Savior and brethren transported to greet,
  While the anthems of rapture unceasingly roll,
  And the smile of the Lord is the feast of the soul?
  MECHLENBERG.

Only Remembered.

1 Fading away like the stars of the morning,
  Losing their light in the glorious sun,
  So let me pass away, gently and lovingly
  Only remembered by what I have done.
  Cho.—Ever remembered, forever remembered,
  Only remembered by what I have done.

2 So in the harvest if others may gather
  Sheaves from the fields that in Spring I have sown,
  Who plowed or sowed matters not to the reaper.
  I'm only remembered by what I have done.

3 So let my name and my place be forgotten,
  Only my life race be patiently run,
  Here or up yonder, I must be remembered,
  Only remembered by what I have done.
  BONAR.

How Beautiful on the mountains. Isa. lii. 7. 8s, 7s and 4s.

1 On the mountain's top appearing,
   Lo! the sacred herald stands,
  Welcome news to Zion bearing—
   Zion long in hostile lands:
    Mourning captive,
   God himself will loose thy bands.

2 Has thy night been long and mournful?
   Have thy friends unfaithful proved?
  Have thy foes been proud and scornful,
   By thy sighs and tears unmoved?
    Cease thy mourning:
   Zion still is well-beloved.

3 God, thy God, will now restore thee;
   He himself appears thy Friend;
  All thy foes shall flee before thee;
   Here their boasts and triumphs end:
    Great deliv'rance
   Zion's King will surely send.

4 Peace and joy shall now attend thee;
   All thy warfare now be past;
  God thy Savior will defend thee;
   Victory is thine at last:
    All thy conflicts
   End in everlasting rest.
   KELLY.

Song of our Pilgrimage. 7s and 6s.

1 O when shall I see Jesus,
   And dwell with him above,
  To drink the flowing fountain,
   Of everlasting love?
  When shall I be delivered
   From this vain world of sin,
  And with my blessed Jesus
   Drink endless pleasures in?

2 But now I am a soldier,
   My Captain's gone before;
  He's given me my orders,
   And tells me not to fear:
  And if I hold out faithful,
   A crown of life he'll give,
  And all his valiant soldiers
   Eternal life shall have.

3 Through grace I am determined
   To conquer, though I die,
  And then away to Jesus
   On wings of love I'll fly;
  Farewell to sin and sorrow—
   I bid them both adieu;
  And you, my friends, prove faithful,
   And on your way pursue.

4 And if you meet with troubles
   And trials on the way,
  Then cast your care on Jesus,
   And don't forget to pray.
  Gird on the heavenly armor
   Of faith, and hope, and love,
  And when you're warfare's ended,
   You'll reign with him above.

5 O, do not be discouraged,
   For Jesus is your friend,
  And if you long for knowledge,
   On him you may depend;
  Neither will he upbraid you,
   Though often you request;
  He'll give you grace to conquer,
   And take you home to rest.

A Parting Hymn. L. M.

1 Come, Christian brethren, ere we part,
  Join every voice and every heart;
  Our solemn hymn to God we raise,
  One final song of grateful praise.

2 Christians, we here may meet no more;
  But there is yet a happier shore;
  And there, released from toil and pain,
  Dear brethren, we shall meet again.

Loving kindness. L. M.

1 Awake, my soul, to joyful lays,
  And sing the great Redeemer's praise;
  He justly claims a song from me.
  His loving kindness, O how free!

2 He saw me ruined in the fall,
  Yet loved me, notwithstanding all;
  He saved me from my lost estate.
  His loving kindness, O how great!

3 Tho' num'rous hosts of mighty foes,
  Tho' earth and hell my way oppose,
  He safely leads my soul along,
  His loving kindness, O how strong!

4 When trouble like a gloomy cloud,
  Has gathered thick and thundered loud,
  He near my soul has always stood,
  His loving kindness, O how good!
                MEDLEY.

The Land of Promise. 6s and 7s.

1 Sinner, go; will you go
   To the highlands of heaven,
  Where the storms never blow,
   And the long summer's given;
  Where the bright, blooming flowers,
   Are their odors emitting;
  And the leaves of the bowers
   In the breezes are flitting.

2 Where the rich golden fruit
   Is in bright clusters pending,
  And the deep laden boughs,
   Of life's fair tree are bending;
  And where life's crystal stream
   Is unceasingly flowing,
  And the verdure is green,
   And eternally growing.

3 Where the saints robed in white—
   Cleansed in life's flowing fountain;
  Shining beauteous and bright,
   They inhabit the mountain,
  Where no sin, nor dismay,
   Neither trouble nor sorrow,
  Will be felt for a day,
   Nor be feared for the morrow.

4 He's prepared thee a home—
   Sinner, canst thou believe it?
  And invites thee to come,
   Sinner, wilt thou receive it?
  O come, sinner, come,
   For the tide is receding,
  And the Savior will soon,
   And forever, cease pleading.

INDEX.

TUNES IN *ITALIC*, FIRST LINE OF HYMN IN ROMAN.

Title	PAGE	Title	PAGE
Always near	5	*Dennis*	77
Am I a soldier of the cross	5	Every knee shall bow	84
Ancient church of God upraising	6	*Evening Song*	94
A charge to keep I have	7	Father, forgive them	14
At midnight's holy hour the saints	12	Father of all, since thou art near	5
As we wend our way to Canaan	13	From every stormy wind that blows	12
Along the tranquil path	15	*Farewell song*	26
America	21	Father, hear me while I'm praying	88
At the grave of Lazerus	23	Fading away like the stars	109
A voice from Macedonia	29	For the honor of our God	97
Almost a Christian	30	From Greenland's icy mountains	34
All the weary and ladened	32	Great God! thy wisdom, power	4
A fisher was out on the lake	50	God, in the Gospel of his Son	4
At Jesus' feet	58	*Growing brighter*	13
All hail! the power of Jesus' name	61	God notes the little sparrow's fall	75
Arlington	63	*Go work for Jesus*	83
Alas! and did my Savior bleed	63	Gently, Lord, O gently lead us	80
Across the silver sea	64	Gird yourself with heavenly armor	77
All things shall work for good	67	God moves in a mysterious way	107
A sweetly solemn thought	67	Gone to the unseen home	105
All truth is one the same	68	Go to thy rest, fair child	103
Agrippa and Paul	73	Hark! the Savior now is calling	48
As in Adam all die	79	Hear the words of Jesus spoken	45
Awake my soul to joyful lays	110	*Hebron*	4
Asleep in Jesus	44	How sweet, how heavenly is the	8
A few more years shall roll	84	*Hope's song*	17
Berea	33	*Home at Bethany*	41
Balerma	75	*Hold the fort*	62
Be up and be doing	90	How firm a foundation	59
Blest be the tie that binds	77	*Heavenly mansions*	92
Be not afraid	102	*Home of the soul*	78
By and by	96	How happy are they	79
Children of the living one	18	Hungry and faint and poor	105
Come, sinners, come to-day	21	How sweet the name of Jesus sounds	95
Children of the heavenly King	19	Hark ten thousand harps and voices	84
Confiding trust	27	*I do believe*	30
Christ's Invitation	32	I'm not ashamed to own my Lord	5
Corner stone	44	In seasons of grief to my God	26
Cornelius	52	I lay at night upon the ground	37
Come, you sinner's, poor and needy	55	In the presence of our God	52
Coronation	61	I'll tell you a story of Jesus	41
Come, humble sinner, in whose	61	I oft have gone by faith to see	70
Come to Jesus	73	I am so glad that Jesus loves me	66
Christ's love for the Church	74	I love thy kingdom, Lord	68
Come, let us anew	85	I came unto him	69
City of God	86	*I will sing for Jesus*	81
Come to Jesus, come	89	I would not live alway	109
Come, Christian brethren ere we part	110	In the Rifted Rock I'm resting	103
Come sing to me of heaven	105	I am waiting for the summons	106
Did Christ o'er sinners weep	7	If you would not be a drunkard	99
Do not say to-morrow	31	I'm but a stranger here	97
Death's river is weeping	40	In all my Lord's appointed ways	44
Dropping down the troubled river	55	In the Christian's home in glory	84

112 INDEX.

Title	Page
Jesus wept	23
Jerusalem, my happy home	47
Jesus loves even me	66
Just across the silver sea	64
Joy to the world, the Lord is come	74
Jesus, lover of my soul	95
Just as I am	44
Keep the path	60
Love divine	16
Look upon us, gracious Savior	44
Lord, what wilt thou have me to do	69
Land ahead, its fruits are waving	76
Let party names no more	105
Lord, while for all mankind we pray	90
Light of the lonely pilgrim's heart	99
Love for all and can it be	97
Martyred Stephen saw the Master	42
My rest is in heaven	41
My hope is built on nothing less	9
Mary to the Savior's tomb	103
Mine eyes have seen the glory	99
My faith looks up to thee	95
My soul be on thy guard	84
My Christian friends in bonds of love	34
Not my will	70
Nearer, my God to thee	67
Now begin the heavenly theme	107
O thou Fount of every blessing	55
O hasten, thou bright morning	54
On the cross see the Savior	14
Oh, when shall I see Jesus	29 110
Obedience	35
O my Lord thou art tender	40
Our God is there	56
Oh, where shall rest be found	68
Oh, what must it be to be there	88
Old hundred	93
Our Father in heaven	94
Only remembered	100
On the mountain top appearing	109
Our souls are in the Savior's hands	101
O for a thousand tongues to sing	95
Oh! think of a home over there	84
Pioneer's song	43
Peace is mine	28
Psalms and hymns and songs	3
Preaching Jesus	10
Pleyel	11
Prisoner's song	12
Prayer for Millenium	54
Perfect unity	68
Preach Christ upon the mount	104
Return, O wanderer, now return	8
Right hand of fellowship	18
River of death	19
Rock of Ages, cleft for me	49
Solid Rock	9
Submission	38
Stephen's vision	42
Second coming	45
Steer straight for us	50
Sweetest thoughts of Jesus	57
Since I can read my title clear	63
St. Thomas	67
Some day at home	71
Sweet bells of memory	87
Safe within the vail	76
Sinner go; will you go	110
Sweet hour of prayer	105
The first song	6
The open door	7
The Lord to Peter gave	7
The Christian's open door	8
The graces of the Christian life	8
Tho' thy path be dark and cold	27
'Tis a funeral song we sing	11
The island	24
The Rock	26
The Savior shed his precious blood	30
The sinners of Berea	33
'Tis not by faith alone	34
The sorrowing bishops around	36
The open grave	37
There is a fountain filled with blood	39
Tenderness	40
Time speeds away	43
Take me by the hand	46
There is a land, a happy land	47
The Savior is calling	48
Through the name	49
'Tis religion that can give	49
'Tis not by words of Moses' law	63
Tho' costly, beautiful, and grand	65
Thy kingdom, gracious Lord	68
Time to sing	72
The Master's footsteps, marked	75
'Tis always new	82
There is a land of pure delight	87
Tallula	91
Trust	80
The rifted Rock	108
Thou art the way, to thee alone	103
Tho' the tempest rages and the day	102
The light of truth is breaking	99
There is light from heaven's portals	98
To-day the Savior calls	97
Tarry with me, O my Savior	84
When I survey the wondrous cross	4
Wessels	15
When first I started on the way	19
What care I for fame's opinion	28
We're bound for the land	53
We speak of the realms of the blest	88
Work and rest	85
What shall I do with Jesus	74
We have heard of a land far away	64
When earth from chaos	56
Webb	29
We yearn for joys we cannot see	75
We are living, we are dwelling	107
When we hear the music ringing	105
What glory gilds the sacred page	103
We're marching on to victory	101
We're hastening at our King's command	100
We are journeying to heaven	96
You may sing of the beauty	59
Years have come and passed away	107

www.ingramcontent.com/pod-product-compliance
Lightning Source LLC
Chambersburg PA
CBHW031619170426

43195CB00037B/1213